DIARY OF A PARTISAN

Rosetta Solari Knox

This is a very short story. A story of long ago when women still wore skirts and there were no jeans; the farmers worked the soil with a hoe; hens in the hen-house went to bed early and from the sky rained guns and ammunitions, hand grenades, English cigarettes and English chocolate. It tells the story of rebels in uniforms of all armies and of an army of wives, sisters, mothers, old men, and children. It is the story of these women who, in spite of fascist and German threats sheltered and fed me; of the guide Gigino, who protected me during the long raids; of the family in Bratto who shared their poor meals with me.

It is the story of our people, our hills and our land under the German occupation.

The year is 1945.

DIARY OF A PARTISAN

Rosetta Solari Knox

AuthorHouse™
1663 Liberty Drive, Suite 200
Bloomington, IN 47403
www.authorhouse.com
Phone: 1-800-839-8640

This book is a work of non-fiction. Unless otherwise noted, the author and the publisher make no explicit guarantees as to the accuracy of the information contained in this book and in some cases, names of people and places have been altered to protect their privacy.

© 2008 Rosetta Solari Knox. All rights reserved.

No part of this book may be reproduced, stored in a retrieval system, or transmitted by any means without the written permission of the author.

First published by AuthorHouse 8/19/2008

ISBN: 978-1-4389-0289-0 (sc)

Printed in the United States of America
Bloomington, Indiana

This book is printed on acid-free paper.

This is an English translation of an Italian MS in the Historical Archives of the Resistance Movement against the Germans in Parma.

Events, places, people are true.

INTRODUCTION

The year 1945 was a crucial year for the Italian Resistance. Mussolini had been forced to resign; had tried to leave Italy; was captured by partisans and executed. The Allies had landed at Salerno. On the path of their advance the Germans had built their strongest line of defense in central Italy in the town and Monastery of Monte Cassino. High on a mountain top both the town and the monastery were built on solid rock and it was here at Monte Cassino that the fiercest battle of the war was fought. The cost of human lives was 350,000; the Monastery and the town were reduced to rubble.

As the Allies and General Eisenhower were advancing in the Po Valley the Italian partisan brigades had reached their largest number. Deserters from the dissolved Italian army, students, stranded prisoners of war, English, Russian, and Australian had joined the movement.

The First Julia Brigade operated at the foot of the Apennines around Borgotaro, a town important to the SS for here was the only track of railroad Parma-La Spezia still in operation.

> For the SS troops the line was the only way out of Italy.
> For the partisans it brought the food supply of the Po Valley.
> Like other brigades the First Julia was autonomous.

PART ONE

It's nice up here.

High up suspended in space very near the sun. Only the mountain peaks are higher than we are. Like us the mountain peaks too seem to shift in the darkening light of evening, they take on an impersonal distant look and seem to fade away. But in broad daylight when the air trembles incandescent like a cloud of dust, the mountains stand motionless in a fluid curve cut against the blue of the sky.

This is our territory.

Our partisan group, the First Julia Brigade, moves between the two banks of the river in a circle, our home town the cosmic central point in the familiar embrace of the mountain range: Molinatico-Santa Donna-Barigazzo in the lower Apennines..

Stationed above the highway we are waiting for the four anti-aircraft trucks. Baffo at one Bren gun, a patrol stationed to his right, one to his left. The other Bren gun is stationed above the Parabolic Bridge where the Germans are working. Battista and his men are on lower ground to our right.

The sun is merciless; our wool shirts are a torment. Eleven o'clock. The hammering on the bridge continues loud and clear. Three Germans are working on the highest iron bars; an unattended submachine gun covers them from the opposite ridge. On the grass near the machine guns are automatic rifles.

At three in the afternoon a runner comes with the information that the departure of the convoy has been cancelled.

It's been a blistering long wait in the cruel heat, and all for nothing. The men sit sullen and exhausted. On the spot Dragotte decides to attack the men on the bridge. He shows Baffo where to place his men; we will join Barbaro at the Bazooka. We are about to move when on the highway we see a German soldier furiously riding a bicycle, he stops, lets the bike drop, waves his arms in our direction, then in the direction of the bridge. The hammering continues but stops at the first burst of the Bren. The three Germans on the high bars scramble down quickly, attempting to seek cover. The gun and rifles on the grass are left useless but from somewhere comes an answer to our fire. We reach Barbaro who immediately fires the first shot of the Bazooka. The roar is tremendous, the counter shot enough to break our eardrums. Now their machine gun rakes the slope in a fan, the bullets fall on the bushes, the soft soil. Our Bren stops firing and they immediately stop firing. Dragotte sends word to Ras and the rest of the men to turn back. In batches, one by one we scramble up the exposed slope of the hill, and drop over to the other side.

A runner reaches us with information that a German car is on the highway. We run to find a place from where to see what is happening. We hear the Bren automatic, Baffo has attacked the car, the car has come to a stop, the driver's door is open, and three German soldiers lie motionless on the tarmac. Another soldier runs toward the side of the road, reaches it, disappears.

Barbaro with the Bazooka on his shoulder, three men and I start out to inform Birichino to prepare a meal. We are all exhausted, dizzy with a day in the sun, eyes and muscles hurting, only the thought of camp and the hope of lying down and sleep keeps us moving.

Under a full moon every tree, every bush has its shadow: at our right we see Lake Bono below us, a flat silver plate. When I think that my knees will give, that I can't move another step, we see in the distance a glow, off and on; the camp fire, we are almost there. Tonight even the tiresome singing voice of Ravella with his eternal Song of the Pilate is welcome.

As we approach, I hear someone say: "she's coming," then another voice adds, "here she is." A woman dressed in black is sitting on the log near the fire. I recognize my mother. I am so tired that my eyes fill with tears. I hug her, let myself drop to the ground near her, place my hand and elbow on her knee as if to pin her down.

It's the first time she has come to see me. On foot, alone.

"I saw where you sleep," she says.

In my absence Jumbo has welcomed her. Now he stays near her and mother looks at him, noticing his wooden crutch. I can imagine what she is thinking: a partisan with only one leg? How is it possible when he has to run? And with only one arm, how can he fire a gun?"

That's what Dragotte said when Jumbo arrived and asked to join.

"For a partisan two legs are not only necessary, they're indispensable, as well as two hands."

But Jumbo stayed, and is among our most trusted.

Mother wants to stay to sleep and Jumbo immediately says: "No, signora, you will not sleep on the straw. I have thought about it, I know where there is a good bed; and you will not return home on foot, I promise."

An hour later Jumbo helps her up on Dora. He places the log near Dora and holds the bridle. Mother sits gingerly sideways on the horse and smiles. I know she would rather be on her feet and walk. Jumbo orders me to tie one of her shoe laces I see is untied.

And so I stand and watch them start out.

On my backpack I find her gift: a pair of rough wool socks she has knitted, the scratchy unbleached socks we all wear, two handkerchiefs made from an old pillow slip, daintily embroidered and a cake of home made soap.

Before dawn the truck arrives to pick us up. We are taking two English Colonels to the last outpost of the First Julia, the telephone cabin at Lozzola. Colonel Baer and his companion (whose name I don't know) don't speak Italian and I have to accompany them to interpret. I will not see mother before she leaves, but I trust Jumbo. He will see that she gets home safely.

On foot we cross a deserted village. Clouds of large flies rise as we walk through the empty main street. Doors and windows are boarded up. A hen perched on the branch of a tree chooses this minute to fly down: She lands among us with a noisy squawk, and, as if offended, takes off noisily.

Around the table in the kitchen we find some partisans trying to knead bread and obviously doing a very poor job. They are covered with flour from their beards to their boots. They slap the dough down roughly on the table and flour rises to cover everything in the kitchen.

But a rich aroma comes from the pot on the stove where a chicken is simmering. On the floor against a wall is a long line of bottles of wine.

"Not bad, not bad at all," says Dragotte "I see that you treat yourselves royally, and all you do is complain."

The observation doesn't convince anyone. Dragotte knows, as everyone else knows, that it's not about the food that the men complain.

In the silence Gherry comes in, the Bren cartridge belt hanging from his shoulder. He drops down against a wall, lets the ammunition belt drop, closes his eyes and is immediately asleep.

Sleep: is there better medicine for sore muscles and burning eyes? Sleep: what every man, every detachment is asking. For a chance to stretch out and sleep. But where can relief come from? From Lozzola to the Pass the territory is in partisan hands. We hold prisoners at Strela, Compiano, and Albareto. In one day eighty Germans were made prisoners at the Pass. Our worst enemy: fatigue, lack of sleep, and the discouragement that comes knowing there is no hope of change: today, like yesterday, like tomorrow. The men are exhausted, the guard to the prisoners is slack, and guards fall asleep on duty.

We continue with the small skirmishes on the highway and on the railway line, knowing that they get us nowhere.

We have pricked a giant monster and we can feel it stir. It stretches, gets ready to strike, we feel it in our bones.

The front is silent.

The Allied advance has come to a stop.

The guide, Gigino, comes for me when it's almost dark. He's a young farmer in Gomel's detachment and I don't know him.
Before leaving on his motorbike Dragotte said: "Gigino knows these hills, he knows how to maneuver here, his home is here. You'll be safe with him."

And it's true. Gigino plods along in the dark at a fast clip. Country people seem to be born with an internal compass; like birds they find their bearings even in the dark and head for where they're going in a straight line.

I follow him as best I can.

We come to a group of farmhouses and Gigino stops before one. It has an outside flight of stone steps. The house is dark. He knocks and for a while nothing stirs. The woman who opens the door looks at us impassively. She doesn't seem happy to see us. She looks at the rifle on Gigino's shoulder, the blanket roll on his other shoulder, gives me a quick glance. In answer to Gigino's question 'can we stop to sleep?' she reflects quite a long time.

"All right, she says, but only if you hide the guns and the signorina changes clothes."

Gigino goes to sleep in the hayloft. I follow the woman to the kitchen where she motions me to a bench and, without another word leaves the room. When she comes back she holds a dress in her hand, a blue rayon dress with white polka dots. "It's my daughter's. It will fit a little short on you."

She sits down on the edge of a chair; in the silence we listen to the loud ticking of the clock on the mantel. After a while she rises. "My son gets up at five, if you like, you can stretch out on his bed."

We are upstairs in the son's bedroom when we hear the sound of the cannon.

We run to the open window and look out. Flashing signals of Bengal lights come from Bratello, Borgallo and San Bernardo.

I take off my boots, stretch out on the bed and immediately fall asleep.

For the Germans this raid is just another operation of war.

Operation Wallenstein 1 and Operation Wallenstein 2. These two divisions that Hitler refused Kesserling on the Allied front are used against the partisan groups in Italy.

A report of the German HQ in Parma reads: 'There are zones threatened by partisans and others in partisan hands. Even in zones already cleared with Operation Wallenstein 1 new bands begin to appear."

Yesterday people woke to the sound of the cannon, followed by the pounding of mortars and then, at six, heavy gunfire from the provincial highway. Today all is quiet.

People continue to arrive, entire families, groups of stragglers, evacuees from the air raids in the cities, all with bags, suitcases, pushing wheelbarrows, carts with the old, the sick or children sitting or lying down on them. They come into the farmyard, after a vacant look around sit down or go to lean their backs against the wall of the house. Still others after a quick look continue on their way. Perhaps they have a place to go. It all happens in a formal silence. The children too are silent, taking their cue from the grownups; they sit with the same serious, solemn expression on their childish faces.

In the kitchen on a wood burning stove a pot of mash for the cows is simmering. The heat is stifling. Women dressed in black with a rosary in their hands sit on two high backed wood benches in front of the stove. They turn and look at me when I enter. The borrowed dress is too short, barely reaches my knees and I feel self-conscious with bare legs. I have rolled my white wool socks over my boots. The women sit expressionless: silent, devoted figures as in a wake for the dead. Each one seems bent on her thoughts of despair and fear.

Fear is contagious, in the room it hangs like a poisonous cloud. Every woman sits closed in herself, starts at every sound: the crackling of the wood in the stove, a shutter outside. Every sound is like a menace, an expectation of disaster.

And suddenly I feel angry, resentful against the partisans, against my brother Gek, against the leader Dragotte. For them I have become a nuisance, a conspicuous parcel they have to dispose of and they have handed me over to a guide. Gigino is with the men, and these women (with good reason) don't want me near them.

In the late afternoon a girl brings the news that one of the German columns has reached Roccamurata, only a few miles from where we are. The heavy firing continues. A woman crosses herself and mutters a Hail Mary aloud.

Dragotte arrives when it's dark. He stops in the doorway and looks around. The unfriendly eyes of the women follow his every move as he leans his automatic Mitra on the wall behind the door and comes to sit where I make room for him.

"How are you doing?" he asks in a low voice.

Still in a low voice he says:

"The SS have entered Borgotaro."

In the silence we hear the crackling of the wood in the stove. I want to ask 'and Gek? did Gek get away?'

"Stop it" he says. Angry, he gets to his feet. "Stop crying." I feel the tears running down my face but I can't stop them.

He sits down again, looks at the nervous opening and closing of his hands between his knees. "Wait here with Gigino, you'll be safe with him. When they have finished cleaning up on the other side of the river, cross over, go to the connection post, your aunt's house. We will come later. Wait for us there."

He gets to his feet, followed by the unfriendly eyes of the women and walks to the door. At the door he turns, makes an uncertain gesture with his hand, takes his Mitra, slips it over his shoulder and leaves.

During the night we are awakened by the barking of the dog. In the crowded kitchen some women are sleeping on the brick floor, some sleep with their shoulders against the walls; there isn't enough room for them to stretch out. I am crouched on one of the wooden benches. On the kitchen table stretched out on a mattress is a woman with a baby in her arms. At the barking of the dog a door opens on the floor above, a light comes on; the dog stops barking, the light goes out and the door closes.

At the first sign of light, I get up and go to sit on a low wall in the yard. A child is crouched against the wall his arms crossed above his head as if playing at hide and seek.

"What are you doing, are you hiding?" He gets to his feet, looks at me. He is about five or six years old, small with wooden clogs on his bare feet. "Where is your mama?" He shakes his head and doesn't answer. Probably his mother is in the wood. It is time for the milking and the cows have been let out of the stables.

In the afternoon another alarm sends the men scurrying for their hiding places.

Gigino comes for me, and we follow the women and children into the woods. The stables have been cleared of cattle and other animals and the wood is crowded with them: hens, goats, cows, big oxen with a wide spread of white horns. The place is a trap, anything can hit you, a cow's horn, a goat might jump at you from a bush, oxen moving with their heavy plunging gait catch their horns in the branches and make a great noise trying to get free. From a bush comes a sudden flutter of wings. With a spiteful squawk a hen announces she's laid an egg.

I stay near women with small children hoping they'll be the first to return home. When a woman with a baby starts walking toward her house, I follow her.

Two girls, Amelia and Renza, come asking for me. They offer to let me share their bed. Amelia refuses to undress. Obviously she is the one who directs operations. I'd like to suggest that if we took turns, if one of us stood guard, the others could get some sleep. But Amelia seems very sure of what she's doing, and I just ask: "Where are the men, where is Gigino?"

"Gigino and the men have a good place, they're perfectly safe. We got it ready for them. It's a tunnel. They slide on their back and when they are all in, we cover with boards and branches. You can't see anything, even if you come right up to it."

"Yes," says Renza," they are perfectly safe…they are buried alive…"

"Don't talk like that, they are safe, that's all that matters. Men come to a bad end in the hands of the Germans."

The dog has stopped barking and we follow Amelia without protest. She leaves the road, stops before some large boulders that hide a deep gully, walks through brambles, rocks covered with moss, we follow. From lower down comes the sound of falling water. When Amelia stops, we choose a stone and sit down.

I have learned to sleep any time, anywhere: sitting, standing, walking. Sleep comes as soon as I close my eyes.

I put my head on my knees, and sleep.

Tonight we will go to sleep at La Rocca, Amelia has decided. Hidden in the curve of the hill it's a small stone hut for drying chestnuts. It can't be seen at ten meters' distance. We find straw on the beaten earth floor and we have brought blankets. I stretch out on my side and immediately fall asleep. When Amelia wakes me, it's still dark outside. They have to get home for the milking, so we start out in the dark.

On the way we meet people going in every direction hunting for a safe place. They follow trails, take shortcuts across fields, meadows, aimlessly retrace their steps, stop uncertain about which direction to take. They know there is no place that is safe.

For the next two nights we go back to sleep at La Rocca. Before dawn once again we start out on the return trip. The road slants down, climbs, and cuts across woods of beeches, pines, and oaks.

This time we take a shortcut to come out suddenly on a wide rock shelf. The edge juts out like the lip of a cliff over the rolling farmland below. A group of women is standing there near a rough wood fence, the only protection against the high drop.

"What are they looking at?" asks Amelia.

A woman turns as we approach. "They are coming."

We walk up to join them where they are standing. Below us we see the head of the advancing German column coming out of the trees. It moves in slow motion, their guns in their hands parallel to the ground, their helmets pushed low over their faces. It's an unreal silence, the silence of nightmares. Like the silence on a screen when the sound track has been cut.

A woman says: "They seem to stand still, they go so slowly."

Another woman crosses herself: "Hail Mary, full of grace…"

"In an hour they are at Barca. "

"If they continue in that direction."

Another woman takes her child's hand. "Come, Nini, let's go."

For me it is a relief to see them, to know in which direction they are heading. Fear is fear of the unknown, fear of the surprise. We stand watching the column sliding like a snake through a meadow, through a wheat field ready for the harvest. Now it's swallowed up between two tall green hedges. Two weeks ago the wild rose was in bloom and a snowfall of pink petals covered the green hedges.

"Amelia cries: Signorina, we have to go."

I turn to follow. Without waiting, she hurries with Renza up the slope. They want to get away from me. I've learned to read people's intentions. No one wants to be found near me.

The other women too are moving way, holding children in their arms or by the hand. The head of the column has disappeared under our feet; the tail is still hidden among the trees. In a short time no one is left but an old man.

He's sitting on a ledge of rock, his hands crossed on a stout stick, his face hidden under an old dusty hat He is completely indifferent to what is happening.

I go and sit down beside him.

In silence we wait for time to pass.

Meal time is a convention, a habit. A habit I have lost. I don't know how many meals I have missed. And I am not hungry. I don't dare ask the farmers for food. I eat what is offered, when it's offered, mostly some bread and cheese or fruit. A few days ago a partisan shared his bread and cheese with me. He had a flask of local wine, rose colored and bitter. I took a swallow and immediately felt it go to my head.

I've caught sight of a cluster of farmhouses on higher ground. I start out in that direction, but I have no intention of going there. I walk to keep moving, not knowing where I am or where I am going.

I follow a gully choked with briars, up a slope of scrubby yellow bracken and the small bells of wild morning glories and puffs of dandelions. Everywhere is the droning of insects, sliding of lizards, hopping of grasshoppers.

I sit down and wait. Time drags in a state of alarm. It seems to come to a standstill. Below by the road the ditches are white with clumps of wild clematis; on the road are stacked piles of gravel… stacks and stacks of gravel stretching away to the turn of the road… stacks and stacks of gravel…

I roll over on my stomach and stretch out full length. I close my eyes, half-asleep, half-awake I see the gravel and the old man with his hammer breaking the stones…the road stretches away to the horizon…now the old man is walking,, his back is turned to me but I know him. He is the old man who, ever since I can remember sat making gravel on the Avenue of Poplars…the sun burns my shoulders, humming, buzzing, whirring of insects and the voice of a school friend:"Do you know what the old man asked his wife when he was dying?"

"No, what?"

"He asked his wife to buy him a pair of new shoes; he wanted to be buried with a pair of new shoes on his feet."

"But why?"

"Because when he was dead he wanted to walk on the gravel he had made. He said to his wife, 'With all the road I have to travel I need a strong pair of shoes on my feet.'" "And did his wife buy him a pair of new shoes?"

"No, his wife said, his shoes were still good and she had them resoled and the old man died happy." The old man died happy, he was tired of sitting making gravel and now he walks...the old man walks on the roads of heaven, that's his job now to walk on gravel...miles and miles of gravel...all the gravel he has made all his life...

When I wake up the sun is higher in the sky. I sit up in the bright glare feeling sick. My head spins, dizzy with heat and hunger. The lizards too lie lifeless in the heat.

Much later I start up the cattle trail in the direction of the houses. The trail crosses a meadow, past a harvested wheat field where a pear tree grows in the middle of the stubble; the stubble is dotted with bright red poppies and larkspur. The houses seem deserted but smoke comes from one of the chimneys. The courtyard of the first house is swept clean, the threshing is over. Beyond the house and stables I can see the untidy litter of old iron, rusty plows, carts, all the discards farmers collect.

From one of the house a door opens and a girl runs out. Without barking, a dog comes bouncing after her from the corner. As she comes near she points to the house behind her. "They've seen you coming."

She adds," They are afraid."

"They are afraid, but I am not."

She stops in front of me. "Can I go with you?"

She smiles, she must be sixteen or seventeen, she doesn't look like a country girl, and her hair is loose down her shoulders, her eyes very bright and cheerful. She smiles, she is glad to see me.

"I know a nice place to hide. I take you there, all right? Wait for me."

She turns and runs toward the house. Again she turns her head and smiles. (Will she bring me something to eat?) When she returns she holds a quilt in one hand and a blanket in the other hand.

"Is it far, I don't feel like walking." I say.

"No, it's not far." I've heard the expression too often to feel reassured. In the country 'it's not far' can mean anything. Kilometers and meters for country people are the same. "How long will it take?"

"You'll see, it's not far, you'll like where we are going." She stops to wait for me

"I have sent my brother to tell Gigino where we are going." Pleased to have thought of everything, she walks with an easy step, turns now and again to wait for me.

She is in love with a partisan, I reflect, for her this is an adventure. She is happy.

We come to a stone hut for drying chestnuts. Placed sideways on the hillside among the trees and underbrush it can't be seen until one comes right up to it. An opening serves as a door, a smaller one as a window. Inside we find dry leaves and twigs and straw on the floor; we gather up the straw and leaves, pile them on the twigs and over them stretch the quilt and the blanket. It makes a soft bed; noisy but comfortable. With a sigh of satisfaction the girl stretches out on her back, crosses her hands behind her head.

"You are right, it's nice here." I close my eyes: "What is your name?" I ask but I don't hear her answer. I am falling, falling into space, sliding into a dark place of blissful well being, I float suspended in a warm liquid, an amniotic fluid that nourishes me. In deep content, I sleep…

A hand shakes my shoulder. "Signorina, look."

"What is it?"

"Fireflies, we have fireflies too to give us light." They come in through openings of the door and window. I close my eyes, I am sleeping, I know I am sleeping. Jealously I hold on to this blessed state, this total eclipse that is sleep. Again a hand shakes my shoulder.

"Signorina, what are those lights?"

I open my eyes but this time it's not fireflies that we see. It is flashing yellow and red signal lights.

The girl asks: "What are they?"

"Signal lights, German signal lights."

We now hear explosions and firing. It's impossible to guess from where they are firing. From everywhere it seems, even from above our heads. Now the repeated bursts have a feeling of urgency. I recognize the heavy pounding of mortars and, muffled by the distance, the burst of hand grenades.

"Let's stay here, we don't know where they are and we are quite safe here."

"No, no, let's go down. Gigino will be looking for you. Let's go down where everybody is."

I understand that her mind is quite set: for her to stay up here means to be cut off from the action, her beautiful adventure can't end up here.

I help her fold blanket and quilt and we start out.

We run into the men at the crossroad, Gigino among them.

I ask immediately. "The column has passed, Gigino, can we stay here?"

"One column, there are two more headed in this direction and we'd be trapped. We go toward Barca while we can."

We have taken our blankets and guns and have thanked the woman. I have returned the dress, and I suddenly realize that the young girl who was with me has disappeared and I haven't even thanked her. I don't even know her name.

It's dark night when we reach Barca and stop at the isolated farmhouse that is Gigino's home. There is no sign of life. In the kitchen Gigino goes for a pillow and a small alarm clock which he winds and places on the floor in front of the bench where I will sleep. He wants me to wake him. "I'll set it for 4 o'clock. We have to get out of here."

It seems I have barely fallen asleep that the alarm rings. The landing and the second floor are dark. I knock on the first door I come to. After a while I knock again, then on the door opposite. From down the hall a door opens and an old woman comes out. She is fully dressed, a long black cotton dress and over it a long black apron that reaches to her ankles. Even the black kerchief on her head is neatly tied. "I'll go and wake him," she says.

When she comes down to the kitchen, she is followed by Gigino who holds a bottle and two glasses in his hands. He pours me a glass of clear liquid; I swallow, choke, and quickly spit it out. "Mamma mia, its fire."
The mother smiles: "No, it's grappa".

"It's an electric shock… it's wakened me completely."

On the way we find that it's still too dark to walk. We are enveloped in a thick fog and even Gigino can't see where to place his feet. Gigino takes first sentry turn. I sit with my blanket over my shoulders close to a hedge on some leaves that are soaked. The fog is beginning to lift, milky strands rise from the river bed, a soft pink flush covers the sky. Behind the hill the sun starts to rise like a red ball. Gigino sits, the blanket over his shoulders, his head thrown back, his mouth hanging open.

On the country road a young mother is walking home holding her ten month old baby girl in her arms. She is unaware of the German sharpshooter in the brush above the road aiming his ta-pum on them.. The danger is past, she thinks, the raid is over, we can go home.

Mother and child are a moving dark object against the bare white dust of the road.

The mother feels the child's blood in her hand, feels the child's body sags in her arms.

The child is dead.

Then, the sound of the ta-pum reaches her ears.

I think of the man who came to the camp asking to speak to me. He had important information for me, he said, standing in front of me with both his hands respectfully holding his hat to his chest. "At Headquarters there is a spy who has promised to hand you over to the fascist Militia. They say they had you but you escaped. This time when they catch you, they say, and they are sure to catch you, you won't get away, so easily this time, they say."

He is well informed on what I am to expect from the fascists. Seeing that I am not impressed, he smiles, an important smile on a mouth with thin lips and a few yellow teeth. It is the smile of someone who knows more than I do. 'They say.' He repeats the words like a rhyme. It crosses my mind that perhaps he is the spy he is talking about.

For some time I have heard the sound of a motorbike on the highway. Now I see it as it turns the corner; through my glasses I distinguish clearly the face of the German driver under the helmet, the closed lips, see the gun on his shoulder, so clear, so close I could touch him with my hand. He drives slowly turning his head left and right, looking up toward the mountain range. In my glasses I follow him to the turn of the road see him disappear. Now I turn my glasses to the farms above the river, to the bridge where we intend to cross. In a clearing lower down on the hillside I see smoke and, near the fire, huddled in a hood made of sacking a man is sitting. His cows move round and round him on their stiff legs as if to protect him.

Now on the bridge I catch sight of a partisan running. His Sten gun is clutched to his chest; he drops off into the underbrush and disappears. I catch sight of him again on the hill, on the road to Belforte. He has made it. Good for him. Now another partisan starts across the bridge. His ammunition belt flapping at his side, he follows the other through the underbrush and up the slope. He too has made it.

The sun has come up, a blood red ball behind the hill.

When Gigino wakes I tell him what I've seen.

We approach a farmhouse and ask for information. At a run we cross to the other side and head for Belforte.

'These Germans are not Christians, said the old woman at Barca, they have no heart. For them we are just animals; they command and expect to be obeyed.'

Her livelihood depended on the sale of her eggs. During the raid the Feldwebel had found the basket of eggs she had hidden and ordered her to boil them. He took them all with him.

Aldo

Dragotte and Rosetta

Gek

Napoli and Ailu

Rosetta and Gang

The Gang

The Author's home

The author

PART TWO

Gigino seems to be as familiar with this side of the river as with the other side. He strides along at a fast clip, now and again turning his head to make sure I follow. High above us, the gray stone houses of Belforte are balanced on the edge of the steep slope and from where we are each house seems to have its feet on the roof of the house lower down.

This is where the SS troops have passed. Farmhouses are now plaster and rubble ruins, fallen walls exposing precariously balanced beds and tables. A man working in a field stops working when he sees us. Both hands on the handle of his spade, he stands motionless looking at us. His farmhouse is a pile of rubble around him.

In June we had stopped at this farm after an attack, we had with us the German and Fascist prisoners we had taken. Then the yard was noisy with chicks, hens and geese. As we started to leave, a careless partisan had fired a shot scattering the lot and overturning a pot of basil on the steps of the house. I see again the scornful sneer on a fascist's face and the expression of indifference on the German faces.

Lower down the hill the road crosses another farm in ruin. Here a man approaches when he sees us. He wears an old straw hat on his head stained with a blue sulfur spray; he holds a pitchfork in one hand. Shaking the pitchfork angrily he says: "So you're back, jailbirds…"and adds: "Haven't you done enough?…."

We go on walking as if he weren't talking to us and his threats, his angry outburst didn't concern us, and we walk along the tall green hedge while he follows on the other side angrily shaking the pitchfork.

Once out of his sight, we stop.
"And now. Gigino?" I ask.
"We're here; we go to your aunt's house as planned."
"I don't think it's a good idea." I answer.
"What else can we do? We might as well find out."
My aunt has been warned. We find a large circle of women gathered in front of her house watching us approach. As we start down the hillside, my aunt breaks away from the women, starts walking toward us.
"They blame me… they say I brought the Germans…they are threatening to burn my house for I am to blame they say…".
She is still talking when we turn around and start back up the hill.
Gigino decides to join Gomel's detachment.
At a loss where to go, I head for Linari, the only place I am familiar with.

I find a place to sleep at Bratto.
It's a poor family with a slew of small children, so many, I can't count them.
"How many are they?" I ask the mother. "Nine." she answers quietly. She is a small gray woman, everything about her is gray: her clothes, her face, the tone of her listless voice. The smaller children are unbelievably wild; they have the dull, apathetic look of creatures that habitually don't have enough to eat. They look at me without any curiosity. They don't know how to play. The older children sleep in some huts that look like sheds; the smaller in a large bed in a room without light. They curl up in a heap in the middle like kittens. The room is stuffy with the odor of closed places, old rags, mice. I sleep dressed on an old sofa against a wall. At night I wake to the whimpering of the children. Perhaps they are hungry. The fleas

in the sofa too are busy and keep me awake. When I can't stand the whimpering of the children and the biting of the fleas, I get up, take my blanket and go out into the woods.

I sit with my back against a tree. This woman has shared with me her poor meals taking the food from the children. I have to do something, contact Gek or Dragotte for food or money some way. Having decided this, I feel better. I roll the blanket around me, stretch out on the grass and try to sleep.
I suspect I will sleep in the open for many nights to come.

During the day the children follow me wherever I go; like chicks around a mother hen they tag along after me, stop when I stop. I go and sit before a stack of lumber and they line up in a semicircle, their eyes fixed on my pistol, my binoculars, and the bill of my wool cap. They are not shy, they are indifferent. Fragile and solemn they stand there in their skin waiting, an uncanny, trance-like waiting, waiting for they don't know what and wouldn't recognize if they saw it.

Tow headed, their untidy hair knows no comb or brush. Their brown skinny faces are the faces of gnomes. Their tight fustian pants the color of dead leaves reach to mid calf. Solemn, ridiculously solemn, small creatures lost in the big forest and perfectly in tune with it. Nothing surprises them.

It occurs to me that in the same way as they look at me now, they must have looked at the German soldiers during the raid. And with the same indifference watched the SS fire their guns into the bushes, search, threaten. The filter of their mind will allow only so much to penetrate, and it is just as well. They are spared ---at least in part.

When I am tired of my thoughts, tired of four pairs of eyes staring at me, I shoo them away. "Go now, shoo, shoo…" They don't budge. "Off with you." I stand flapping my arms like a mother hen flapping her wings.

Without turning their head they take two steps back and stop. If I don't move, they will not move.

One night I am awakened by the sound of a plane. I recognize the sound of the airlift plane and fall asleep again certain that Gomel and his men will have listened to the messages from London. The plane comes back the next night, leaves, and comes back. At Prato Piano the holes are ready, the wood stacked ready for lighting the prescribed fires. When the plane comes back the third night, I expect Gomel and his men. Instead it is Emma, Maria, and their father who come.

Emma asks in her abrupt way: "Do we light the fires?"

The electric power doesn't reach Linari and I ask: "But you haven't heard the messages?"

"This is the third night, Gomel and his men are probably on the way."

While we are talking the plane returns, circles above our heads lower and lower; leaves, comes back.

We go to Prato Piano and light the fires.

There is no drop.

A young girl comes looking for me with some news to tell me. "The Militia entered your house, threw a lot of your books out of the windows into the garden, made big piles and tried to set them on fire. Do you want to go and look?"

I have orders not to approach Borgotaro and I hesitate.

She waits and smiles hopefully. "I can lend you one of my dresses…"

I accept and we start out.

The road drops all the way under the chestnut trees and it's a short, pleasant trip. We are close to the railway station when on the bridge we see three German soldiers leaning on the iron railing of the bridge holding a hand over the strap of their ta-pum slung over their shoulder.

A woman comes out of a house and walks toward us wiping her floury hands on her apron.

"Signorina, don't be foolish, please, please don't let them see you, the patrol is about to start out on its round."

"What patrol?"

"It starts from the station, goes through the center of town and comes back along the walls every morning about this time. You can't reach your house without meeting them."

I turn to the girl: "It was a stupid idea anyway, let's go back."

"Let me go and look. Since we're here, I'll go and walk past your house"

When she returns she shakes her head.

"There was a notice on your garden gate, but I couldn't read it, it's in German."

One day I returned to Linari.

Step by step along the trail the SS troops followed in the raid, through the same underbrush under the chestnut trees, the same green silence. The three stone huts where more than sixty partisans had lodged were empty, cleared of even the straw matting on which they slept. The SS had made an effort to burn them; on the beaten earth floor of the middle hut were left the remains of the fire, burnt stumps and cinders and above them the heavy ceiling beams were blackened by smoke. It was a half hearted attempt. Stone walls and slate roofs don't burn easily, so they had given up.

By the dry wall were the remains of the fire for the cooking pot; not far way the spring flowing in a thin stream out of big boulders. I remember that the water was so cold it had a taste of metal.

The brick and stone oven was still standing. Perhaps the SS didn't know that the partisans had built it. Knee high weeds, ferns, stinging nettles have taken over the vegetable garden; high on a cherry tree were still some ripe cherries, out of reach.

Linari before the June raid was like no other place. Linari was a state of mind. It was the beginning of the Resistance and we were still a few.

Now it's still the same Linari, but nothing is the same. It has the desolate air of a place no longer being used.

This is what is most frightening about the SS. Where they pass they lay waste with mechanical thoroughness. Impersonal, devastating, they make sure nothing is left standing. They leave behind an air of suspense, of waiting. One can't believe they are really gone.

The army had broken up with the fall of Mussolini. The railway system was choppy, trains ran for short distances, were full of army deserters and students taking to the hills.

The fascists called us "Outlaws" "Rebels" The Germans called us "Banditen".

Linari is high country, up here the air is thin, and one has to learn to breathe at this height. Too high for growing wheat or grapes, it's a land of shepherds and soft coal makers, charcoal burners. The men, tall and lean, look like peasants but are not suspicious like peasants. They own no land, cattle or harvest. Their life too is hard, but their needs are few. The women are reconciled to their life and go about their work mild and serene. The children are born old, small adults with responsibilities; they speak only when they are spoken to, and address their parents with the old-fashioned polite 'Voi'.

Armed with long sticks each morning the children start out before dawn with their flocks. They go to gather other flocks of sheep and goats to drive them to pasture to Noli and Zeri, and higher ground in the Apennines. Up there under that open expanse of sky they stay all day long, wild and free as their goats.

Unlike the farmers the shepherds accepted the arrival of the partisans in silence, without protest, as they would accept an act of God, a blizzard or some other natural disaster. The partisans were no trouble; they took care of their own food supplies, built an outside oven to bake their daily rations of bread, and were relaxed and friendly. They brought a glimpse of the outside world, another life exciting to the two girls, Emma and Maria.

For the partisans it was a kind of regression into a slower, more primitive existence. We felt at home, part of a new family high in the mountain ranges. Out of reach of fascists and Germans, we were safe.

Or so we thought.

The reality Linari as it is now doesn't cancel the reality Linari as it was then. Circumstances have changed, men have changed. For me it was here that it all started.

I was wanted by the fascists and I was hiding at my aunt's house, a house the partisans used as a connection post, when a school friend, Punteria, came and asked me: 'Would you like to join?' I gave it no second thought, he is joking, I thought, I'd never heard of a girl in a Brigade. But Punteria was not joking, he had (with Ailù) made plans, and I was part of them.

The plan was to enter the railway station and pick up the patrol just before the commuter train started from the station at 5.30 am.

Ailù is the one who brings me a gun, a Beretta, and shows me how to fire it,

The first night we have no luck. Reconnaissance planes come circling above the station and the railway bridge and bring out the guards. From our hiding places we listen to their talk and decide to turn back.

On the second try things go better. We stop for a meal at a wine shop where we leave the mules. I count jealously the glasses of red wine Ailù pours. It's still dark when we leave. We stop in a ditch and Ailù sitting beside me immediately falls asleep.

The strike was Punteria's idea. He had all the information on the two guards, school friends of his. His plan was just to teach them a lesson, to make them undress, say a prayer on their knees and send them home in their underwear.

Dragotte, the leader, knows nothing of all this.

Punteria, Tuono and Renzo will follow the railway tracks to keep a lookout for the patrol. Ailù and I will enter the station and pick up the two guards.

A big blonde moon rides high above our heads, every building, every tree, every bush has its shadow. Ailù, now awake starts swearing: "Who invited you….who needs you tonight of all nights, you bastard……" For a moment I think he is referring to me, but with each swear word he shakes his hand at that impudent moon riding high above our heads.

We find the platform and the waiting rooms partially darkened for the curfew, an old soldier sits on a bench on the platform waiting for the train, his rifle across his knees, his suitcase beside him. Ailù quietly approaches him, lifts the rifle off the man's knees, and the man finally lifts his head and, seeing Ailù's beard, shows a glimmer of awareness.

"Where are the guards?" Ailù asks.

"In the first class waiting room." The man answers.

Ailù motions me to go. I knock on the first class waiting room door.

"Sartori, open the door."

"Who is it?"

"It's me."

"Who me?"

"Don't you recognize me?"

Ailù, with the Militia man, has followed me and pushes the door and turns the light on. As we had expected, they are two stretched out on benches. Now they sit up wide awake.

Ailù goes straight to the clothes rack where some rifles are hanging. I see belts and munitions on the mantel; still the two men seem unable to move. Roughly Ailù pulls them to their feet, pushes them out of the door out on the platform past the few sleepy passengers waiting for the train all unaware of what is happening.

We hurry them through the station entrance, across the parking lot, down the slope to the highway.

It happens all so quickly and smoothly, it is as if we had rehearsed it.

On the highway Ailù lets out a piercing whistle to inform the others.

And under that full blonde moon we feel masters of the world, lords of the universe.

We are bursting with happiness, an uncontrollable need to shout, dance for sheer joy. Proud and happy, we push the three men before us, up the hillside to higher ground. When the others join us, we let Punteria take over. He orders the prisoners to undress and we stand watching them tear the hated black shirts off their backs and pull off their pants. Then Punteria orders them to kneel and say a prayer for having been 'liberated'.

"Idiots, let this be a lesson. Go home, think about it and come to your senses…"

It's the old man who first becomes aware of what is happening at the angry tone of the order:"On your feet."

"Get on your feet." Ailù repeats. Still kneeling, the old man holds out his extended hands: "I am a married man, I have children……I beg you."

Punteria still talking finally is aware of what is happening. "Ailù…"

"We were agreed, Ailù. It was just a lesson, we were agreed… Ailù…"

He goes on: "Ailù, Corrado is my friend…it was understood, it was just a lesson….we were agreed…" He can't stop talking. "Corrado is just a stupid idiot who likes strutting around in a uniform…Ailù."

"Too bad, he has finished strutting around…."

I am standing next to Ailù, with an instinctive shove I push my elbow against him, turn the direction of his gun. Ailù grabs my arm, twists it roughly. Again he pulls it down and twists it around.

"Don't ever, ever dare…you hear, don't ever dare to interfere with my pistol…he pushes his bearded face against my face…you hear? Don't ever come anywhere near my gun."

Punteria can't stop talking. "Corrado is my school friend…"

We have come down to earth.

Renzo and Tuono have not moved or said a word.

"Run, idiots run…" I see the old man's watch and chain on the grass; I pick it up and throw it after him. He bends, picks it up and runs.

Mechanically we gather up guns, ammunition, belts; leave uniforms, torn shirts and fascist hats on the grass, and silently head back to pick up the mules and supplies.

We are still in shock when we head for Linari.

Dragotte, Corrado and Gek have heard about it even before we arrive at camp.

"Idiots, idiots, idiots …do you realize what you have done…… what is going to happen now…?"

Dragotte and Corrado take turns shouting, threatening….but I am not listening….

I am in heaven…I did it…I did it…. a voice in my head repeats…. You're here…you did it, you did it.

I was so anxious to join the brigade, anxious to be one of them that I had forgotten one thing: I was afraid of the woods at night, afraid of the dark.

For me the wood was not the mythic forest of elves, gnomes and fairies of northern tales, it was not Dante's dark wood of the infernal region, for me it was a world peopled by family ghosts. It was mother's bedtime stories….a nebulous country of fogs where dead men don't rest in peace but come back to interfere with the living. Family ghosts who come back to settle old scores, pull people out of bed. All the bedtime tales we had listened to shivering with delight. They were stories that that left us children for ever afraid of the dark. I thought of them. They were still there these restless ghosts but to my surprise they were no threat. It was a separate world under the chestnut trees. The darkness was no threat. Day and night the wood was the same wood.

A chestnut wood is a wood without light. Branches meet overhead and through the tangle of leaves light spills down in pin points. There are no flowers in the sparse underbrush, just a few maiden ferns and some low plants of whortleberries. Trails suddenly appear and as suddenly disappear. Walking in the morning in that green twilight is like walking in the bottom of the sea. Then in an opening of the trees suddenly a long stretch of grass appears, tall dark green blades tipped with blue flowers, in long stretches that wave in shimmering fluorescent waves.

At this height wheat doesn't grow. The staple is chestnut flour, not wheat. Large flat pancakes baked on chestnut leaves under the hearthstone. It has a particular new taste, new to most of us.

In the evening the family comes together for supper. They sit on two benches on either side of a long deal table in a bare whitewashed room. Elbows on the table, the men with their hat on their heads, the family sits in absolute silence. They eat plates of pasta made of chestnut flour.

In a corner of the table I sit with my bowl of milk and the bread that I have kept of my ration.

The partisans have built an outside oven of brick and stone. Here the daily ration of bread is baked: a small loaf for each partisan. It is heavy, dark and delicious.

Maria and Emma have made room for me in their bed. As if afraid of touching me, they lie down on the very edge of the mattress, a mattress of dried chestnut leaves, noisy and soft. During the night they roll against me to the center of the bed and I sleep hedged in by Maria, robust and soft on one side and Emma all bones on the other. When I wake up, I find they have left.

The white washed room has no furniture; some clothes hang from nails on the walls. The window is a square small opening in the stone wall with no curtains.

It is a room of spare Spartan simplicity.

Now that I am here, if I think that I belong, that I am one of them, I soon find out I fool myself. Gek's and Dragotte's promises are just to keep me quiet. Neither has any intention of keeping them. I receive the rations each partisan receives: a loaf of bread, cigarettes, wine, if I want it, and an English army shirt and pants.

One night they leave without me. I feel humiliated.

A patrol stops them at a bridge. After an exchange of fire they turn back. They will try again tonight. And I will be one of them.

Lupo, a born organizer has collected information and assigns each of us a task: Gek and I will go to pick up two spies, a woman and a man. The others will pick up some evacuees suspected of trafficking in guns and ammunitions.

To cross the river, because of the patrols on the highway, we make a long detour. We leave the two mules at a safe distance and approach with care. It's a very large solid apartment building of many floors. Ailù and Gek approach the front door and knock. A light comes on, a window on the ground floor opens and a man's head appears a grizzled old man's head. Immediately some shots whiz past his ears. The head disappears, the window is quickly closed; shouting and confusion.

"Who's the idiot who fired?" Now everyone dashes forward, jostling and pushing to get through the front door.

"Keep that gun lifted," Ailù points to my gun, and points to a door down the hall. 'That door....' Gek motions me to do as I'm told. I approach the door and push it open.

The room is almost completely filled with two large beds where many children are sitting up alert and fully awake. They are evacuees from the air raids in the city. They look with interest at us, at me, my gun, my cap, at the partisans pushing in after me. A small boy looks at me again and asks; "But aren't you a girl? Why do you wear pants?"

Near him is sitting an old woman who asks calmly: 'And what do you think you're doing bursting in here like this?'

A partisan approaches a heavy trunk, (we are looking for a trunk containing guns). He plunges his hands in and extracts handfuls of women underwear, silky pants and bras. Laughing he holds them up, lets them drop back in the trunk and again holds them out.

"Here are the guns you have come for, help yourself."

Later we find ourselves outside, confused and embarrassed. And amused too.

"Now what?"

We have not found the two spies. We found no guns, but someone has appropriated two bottles of wine. Now he holds one up and asks: "Anyone with a bottle opener?"

"Who needs a bottle opener?" Ailù takes the bottle, breaks the neck against the entrance step of the building, tilts his head back and drinks.
"Brindisi."
"To the last honest man."
"If one still exists."
He passes the bottle to Gek who tilts his head back and drinks.

And to think I had looked forward to this…

In the evening the partisans gather in the shepherd's kitchen for the evening entertainment. The kitchen, a room with low ceiling and heavy smoky beams is lighted by an acetylene lamp; two high backed wooden benches and a third bench between them face the open fireplace. The performance consists of stories about important fascists we all know.

Like gossipy women, the men are having fun. They know the most intimate details of these town people: the life of the pompous bureaucrat, the secret doings of the arrogant small despot. They know bedroom details intimate enough to make anyone listening squirm. How do they know them? Are they true?

The old woman spins in her corner, the twist breaks in her hand and the spindle rolls at our feet. The two small boys sit on the edge of their seat as on seats in a theater, they don't miss a word.

We have two born comedians: Saga and Renzo. Tonight they give us a fresh performance: a meeting between Mussolini and Hitler. Seated at a small table, they lean forward and shout at one another. Like angry dogs they communicate with guttural barks…. the pose, the stance, the tone are just right: they are Hitler (two fingers smoothing his non-existent mustache) Mussolini (jaw thrust out) they bark out empty sounds, fierce growls without uttering a word of Italian or German.

The old shepherd sitting stiff-backed in his corner breaks out in a smile.

The raids are over.

Gek and Dragotte are at Gomel's camp and send a messenger for me. We will cross the river after dark. The new camp is at Malarino. When we meet we look ill at ease. Our faces gray, drawn, hollow eyed as after a long orgy. Dragotte shows the strain of the past weeks; thinner, eyes sunk deeper than ever in their sockets. All of us are ragged and dusty. Some men are in civilian clothes having got rid of their uniforms during the raids.

We are eight with two mules. German patrols still move on the provincial highway and we make a wide detour. The hooves of the mules make an infernal noise on the blacktop of the highway. Ailù and three men cross on the mules, the rest of us sit down and take off boots and stockings, roll up our pants and cross in a shallow spot. I put my foot on a slippery stone that rocks and my foot lands in the slimy mud. Dragotte laughs and immediately lands with both feet in the muck. All of us burst out laughing.

We are in a mood to laugh for no reason. It's a catharsis. We are alive and together. It's the simple joy of finding ourselves alive.

Here's the paradox: because of their brutality against the helpless and innocent, the Nazi-fascists have pushed us closer together. They have dispersed the last doubts or feelings of guilt we might still hold in this civil war we wage against brothers.

Sitting on a sandy bank we dry our feet and put on our boots. The mules have long disappeared among the trees on the slope. From the river bed comes the concert of frogs and crickets.

On the way Dragotte points out the gulch in which they hid on two occasions.

"After they passed, we went back to the same camp. Who would have expected them back? The second time was a close shave: we hardly had time to gather our stuff and run. For sure it was the work of an informer."

Near camp a voice challenges us, we recognize Baffo's voice and we answer with loud shouts and laughs.

We are exhausted, but no one wants to sleep. There are too many things to discuss, to talk about. Fumo tells his tale (he is sixteen, the youngest), the men listen, he closes his eyes and falls asleep sitting up. Gek winks at me. "Our hero is played out."

It is an enchanting night full of stars. Thick shrubs and trees close us in with protecting motherly arms: we are a relaxed happy circle. We are happy to be together again -- happy to stare into the bright eye of the fire -- happy to be alive. For me it's a new experience, being with them, with Dragotte.

On the other side of the river, above the rounded hump of Molinatico a star winks like a signal, on and off.

A group of 120 SS troops starts from Berceto on a surprise attack of the Divisional Partisan HQ.

The guide is someone sympathetic to us partisans. Following him the SS march all night long until ten the following morning. The guide is stalling, praying for a miracle, he leads them all night through long tortuous trails.

The miracle did not happen: the surprise was complete.

First to fall were the sentries: Boeri, Settimo, and Enzo.
Next to fall was the contact officer: Penola.
The commander Pablo was next to fall, his Mitra jammed.
Last to fall was Renzi, the Staff Commander.

Quiet days.

Baffo has left on patrol with three men. Birichino has scoured the iron pot at the spring with a handful of sand. Saga has washed his socks and is stretching them out to dry on a bush. A semi circle of men is sitting playing cards. Gek holds a few cigarettes in the palm of his hand and counts them.

Dragotte grumbles: "You are all sitting here doing nothing and Ailù has gone alone to pick up the bread?"

The German anti-aerial station is not far from the house where our bread supply is delivered. The German patrol, always two men, always follows the same route; our patrol has kept them under observation and is not worried.

It's a day of calm. Ailù has left before daylight with a mule. Boris and Birichino have prepared the food. When the men line up with mess tins and plates we notice that it isn't Ailù dishing out the ration. The line moves unevenly, stops. An argument breaks out. When Ailù is at the pot the line moves smoothly. He doesn't lift his eyes from the plate on which he dishes out an equal portion and the line moves on. There is no arguing.

I like to watch Ailù prepare the food. He moves with the economy of gestures, the precision of an expert cook. Now with special care since every morsel of food has become precious. And what he serves us is always well prepared.

Ailù was an Alpino, now he is a cook and muleteer; stocky, heavy shouldered, short neck, thick eyebrows. His ferocious look is due to the thick black beard that covers almost all his face. Where has he taken his partisan name? It is a flight of wings, of grace as fragile and strong as the side of his nature which he hides, as if ashamed, under his rough manner. Ailu looks his part; on his shoulder he carries his rifle, an automatic '91, later he would leave alone one night to pick up a fascist to get his Mitra for the Mitra is the one automatic weapon every partisan wants. At his belt he carries two Sipe hand grenades, his pistol and the ammunition belt. His inseparable hat has taken the shape of his head. If he takes it off to wipe his face, one can see the line straight and sharp that cuts his forehead in two parts, the white forehead from the lower part of his face.

Nobody saw him arrive. We find him among us, breathless and shaken after the steep climb, and see immediately that something has happened.
"Where's the mule?" someone asks. "And where is your rifle?"
"What happened to you?"
Ailù, mortified, his thumbs in his belt looks down at his boots.
"Leave him alone." says Dragotte.
Ailù goes to sit on the cabin step. Boris brings him bread and cheese, pours him a glass of wine. Some of us sit down; others stand in a semi circle waiting. We feel the agitation, the scare he's still under, each one of us thinks 'I could have been in his place'. It's a smothering feeling, the sensation that we are never alone -- the fear of surprise.
"This time they got you, old man, you and your pistol."
"No, it's Max who is talking," he had only the rifle and the bayonet, he didn't have his pistol."
"Where did they catch you?" asks Dragotte.
"I was talking to some evacuees waiting for the bread that hadn't come yet. I didn't see them, I felt the gun against my back and saw everyone around me move quietly away, women, children, everyone. The one holding the pistol slips the rifle off my shoulder and gives me a shove and turns me around. The other slips my bayonet from my

belt. He turns it round and round before his eyes, laughs and shows it to the other. It's sharp all right, I keep it razor sharp, he holds it up against my chin, and I think damn the fellow now he's going to shave my beard off. Instead he says: "You, grosso bandito." I am big? They were big, hefty fellows; I don't come to their shoulders. One wears shorts, that one puts out a hand and, before I know it, grabs a handful of beard and gives a sharp pull, God damn him to hell, what does he think he's doing…raus rus ach ach, they sound like biting dogs, they're having the time of their life. They think they've landed a big frog. One gives me a shove, then another, they push me down the hill to the road. They don't know it yet but I know for sure…. they won't take me alive. With a grinning giant on one side of me, another on the other and me in between, and between two thick hedges there's not much I can do. We come to the turn of the road, up ahead I see a small bridge, I think this is it, now or never and I get ready. When we are near the bridge I lift my elbows, bang as hard as I can, I hit my elbow into one, then the other, see them fall back and away I go. I jump into a culvert…."

He stops, looks at the empty glass in his hand, he is at the bridge and we are too… running jumping, running with him our heart in our throat.

He goes on. "There was a vineyard, corn plants in between the rows, I rush into it like a mad bull…. break every plant in my way; I can hear bullets singing around me. When I take time to turn my head, I see the one wearing shorts firing his pistol; he doesn't scare me at that distance, but the other, the other is no fool. On his knees, his eye is on the sight of the ta-pum, I run cold, when they take aim, they don't miss. The shot is like a cannon shot, it came too close, if he aims again, I am done for. I zigzag like a mad bull, I don't look back. But by now I am near the trees and I know he can't get me."

As Ailù is talking, we see the mule with the sacks of bread making its way up the slope, Teo leading him. When he approaches, Teo stops, stares at Ailù as if seeing a ghost. After a while Ailù notices him.

"Well, have you never seen me before?" He looks at the two sacks of bread on the mule. "What are you waiting for, for me to unload for you?"

German patrols return to the village, the corporal in shorts and others. They search houses, stables, threaten, shout at the women and old men. Little do they guess how close the 'big bandit' is. He is just a short bird's flight away from them. Through my binoculars I watch a woman in a vegetable garden near a house gather green beans in her apron. She's almost hidden by the tall support sticks. On the other side of the river the tip of the mountain range is clear cut in the soft green light of evening. Candidus is watching the group of card players. Max stokes the fire, Ailù watches him.

Ailù is home and all is well.

A sudden alarm makes us move. The huts are well placed, hidden in a thick wood of locusts and beeches but the position is low, easily accessible to surprises. Barbaro opens the march, the Bazooka on his shoulder; Volpe comes after him with the heavy 20mm. We go slowly.

Walking has become a pleasure. The first kilometers loosen the leg muscles, and then moving become easy, hypnotic: up and down the legs move rhythmical like pistons. Now we could go on for ever in a hypnotic trance, sleepwalking.

Only Gek doesn't appreciate long marches. He counts the miles gone, the ones to come. At the first rest he takes off his boots and socks to massage his poor swollen feet. His feet are of collective interest, we know it will take pleading and threats to persuade him to get up.

"Come on, get moving, Gek."

Gek doesn't hear, he concentrates on the sole of his liberated foot stroking it tenderly. He takes the clean socks I keep for him in my pack and ignores everyone's impatience. "Come on, Gek, says Il Moro, get up." Finally Corrado, hands on hips, stops in front of him. 'Damn it, get to your feet."

"Go on, go, who's holding you?" Gek makes a generous gesture with his hand in all directions, horizon included. "What are you waiting for, go."

Eventually the good Lord, who moves the moon, moves Gek too. Condescending, slowly Gek puts on socks and boots and the column can start out.

Ermeleto

The new camp is even better. It's a stripped bare crown on the mountain bluff where the sun beats straight down. It's open to a vast expanse of sky, today drained of all color, it's a silver radiance, and it's like breathing luminous air. At our feet the land drops off in scattered small farms, fields, meadows, vineyards. The town is spread out along the river; almost parallel to the town are the railway tracks and the provincial highway.

Looking down to our eyes hill tops and slopes rise out of the mist like the ribs of a monster skeleton.

This is poor land, sharecroppers' land where skinny cows pasture in the vineyards.

The camp consists of two rooms. In the first room the open fireplace runs the length of one wall. Water is a problem. The spring is a thin flow that has to serve for cooking and washing up. It has to supply drinking water for the horses and mules too.

We are eight sleeping on the parachute. Our knapsacks serve as pillows. Gek travels light; I keep for him spare underwear in my pack so he can change.

Captain John sleeps with his boots on (ready to move or because he doesn't trust us?) Obstinately English, he keeps to himself and we respect his privacy. We don't know much about him. Only that his plane was shot down and that he has chosen to stay with us. He speaks Italian badly; the few words he uses have a strange sound to our ears making us think that Italian is not a language for everybody. He knows I speak English but doesn't encourage me to speak it.

Sometimes he leaves the camp on a mule, invited to tea by some ladies who speak English. His back straight, his long legs dropping down on either side of the mule, his feet almost reach the ground. He is tall, fair of hair and skin, his uniform as dusty and worn as ours, but in contrast to ours his appearance is military and dignified. He is always grumbling, muttering in English to himself.

This morning the sky is a pale wash of blue and by mid day the shimmering light is so strong it hurts our eyes. We hear a burst of gunfire down the hillside. Candidus goes to see who fired.
"An idiot fired at the farmer's dog."
"What for?"
"It stole a piece of cheese from him."

It is nice to be back among familiar, trusted faces, to hear again familiar expressions, to see Corrado lost in thought fastidiously smoothing his moustache, to listen to Max and Ailù sharing a story. They laugh a lot, Max and Ailù; they have in common a merry sense of the absurd.
Looking at them, I reflect, they are in their element.

During the night I woke and found the room full of moonlight. It came through the openings of the door and window, left dark shadows around the walls, covered the sleeping men and their guns. High, intense it came like an SOS, a warning. To my eyes the sleepers seemed exposed, fragile, and defenseless. Guns, grenades, a whole arsenal of arms are of no use in a surprise.
They are all vulnerable, and myself even more vulnerable. I am vulnerable and exposed -- a girl among men. My priorities have shifted: social pressure, public opinion, home, family, and school… another life. It's a strange experience, this strange life that is becoming no longer strange.
Every day is fresh and new. It is nice to wake at night, feel Dragotte near, to listen to his breathing in the darkness, soft and steady among the breathing of the other sleepers. It is nice to close one's eyes and imagine tomorrow, another day in the perfection of these days.

The familiar sounds of the awakening camp, the dawn patrol leaving, the stamping of the horses, the smell of smoke as Birichino starts the fire. Max brings the fresh milk he's gone to buy at the farm.

We sit up on the parachute, straws in our hair -- the dissipated look of persons who sleep in their clothes and don't wash much, mess kits at our feet. We cut the left-over ration of bread into the milk, and Corrado adds sugar by heaping spoonfuls, Ras wants it heated. Dragotte laughs at me: "Look at her; she breaks the bread into the milk as if she were crumbling it on a window sill for the birds."

We have lost track of time: what day is today?
When we go outside to see the morning, the foothills are still hidden; the mist rises like long streaks of skim milk from the river. The bells of San Pietro start ringing for mass.
It is Sunday.

When I take my basin of water I go to a shed to wash, I find a goat perched on the slate roof, balanced on the gray tiles she seems to be waiting for me (ready to attack or to run?) She lowers her head, and then looks at me with yellow wicked eyes. There's something infernal in the looks of this animal all knots and sharp angles, so skinny and hungry who never stops eating, and is always hungry. There is something diabolical in her sharp little beard, curved horns and shrill bleating. I hurry inside and hear her stamping on the roof trying to look through the broken tiles. She is curious as well.

We are on patrol; on the other side of the river we can see the roofs of the tanning mill, the railway station, the railway tracks and the bridge. About this time every afternoon the bomber Pippo appears; the English Spitfires come at night, the American Mustang and Fortress pass by day, but Pippo comes by day and by night. If he catches the least point of light at night, he pounces and starts firing.

The bridge brings them, the single track of railroad Parma-La Spezia that crosses the Po valley. They come, circle high above, glide, drop their load, swerve abruptly to miss the hill, and rise with a shriek of rage. The stone piers of support, broad and solid, hold up the single iron track, and from up here through binoculars, the track spans the river in a beautiful curve, an elegant curve that seems a marvel of the art of engineering. When the roar of the planes has died, the dust and smoke cleared, we see on the pitted bed of the river uprooted willow bushes and large holes that fill with water. The bridge stands.

It will be difficult to hit it directly.

Lupo makes his appearance at camp now and again but doesn't stop. He makes war on his own, wants to impress and astonish; in civilian clothes he infiltrates the enemy's ranks, causes confusion, doesn't accomplish very much, but is well informed on enemy movements. He carries out coups on his own; firmly convinced he has a charmed life. 'His motto Providence loves the brave'. When a German staff car surprised a group of partisans before a hotel, in the shooting that followed Lupo wearing civilian clothes, grabbed the handle of the grenade from the surprised German officer and just threw it.

No civilian no German or partisan was hurt, proving as he insists; he is under Providence's special care. He has had the closest escapes of anyone.

"Let's go and watch Corrado make himself pretty," says Dragotte.

On the hillside below us Corrado is crossing a meadow on his way to the farmer's house, a towel across his shoulders, and a cloth bag in his hand.

Holding hands we start down the slope at a run that threatens to land us on our faces. Below us Corrado proceeds with military dignity.

These morning ablutions take place in the peasant's kitchen, a spacious room with two large windows of four panes each. Mariulen has taken a basin of warm water from the woman's hands, placed it on a kitchen chair near a window. A small shaving mirror hangs from a nail in the wall. A little girl hides her face in her mother's skirt, but peeps out with one eye; the farmer has stopped on the open door to watch. Corrado, in no way embarrassed by the spectators, proceeds with method. He soaps his chin, his cheeks, leans toward the mirror, starts shaving his right cheek, then his left. When he is done Mariulen takes the basin and throws the soapy water out of the door. With a glass of water Corrado brushes his teeth, opens his lips and admires his teeth, white and beautiful. In silence we follow all his moves. Now he places a boot on the kitchen chair, starts to brush one boot furiously, and then the other one. Now he straightens, fastens his belt and holster, adds to it two Sipe grenades and hangs his binoculars around his neck. With his elbow he gives his Alpino hat a quick brush, straightens the feather to the correct angle.

"How refined you are." says Dragotte. Indeed Corrado in every way looks and behaves like an ideal Alpino

Dragotte snaps to Mariulen: "Attention. The Vice-Commander is ready to assume his duties." And turning courteously to Corrado he asks:" Shall we go to inspect the cavalry?"

"A good idea." says Corrado seriously.

The cavalry consists of two horses and three transport mules.

Corrado doesn't look like a partisan; he doesn't sleep with his hat on, and hasn't lost his civilized habits. To someone he heard laugh at Giorgio for wearing pajamas, he commented:"What is so funny? Why does it amuse you if Giorgio wears pajamas? We can still be civilized, can't we? And here is something else I don't understand, we are the Commando, agreed? Then why can't we be treated like officers, sit at table like officers, follow the protocol, behave like officers?"

The burst of laughter that greeted this remark was so loud and prolonged that Corrado, for once, was dismayed. He never mentioned table service again.

Corrado's line of conduct is straight forward: a partisan is a soldier, his duty is to fight for his idea, fight to win, not die. The fascist mystique that glorifies death is nonsense. Corrado is a veteran of a long campaign in Greece so he doesn't forget that he is vice-commander and behaves accordingly. But this does not change anything, his long and fussy tirades, his insistence on discipline are out of step, they disperse into the open unheeded. They are too close a reminder of fascist fanaticism and German robot discipline.

In the hills we change. Almost without being aware of it, everyone changes in his own way, some more than others. In this collective experience of affinities and contrasts, family connections, there are no rules, laws, maxims and each one of us behaves according to his nature. And each metamorphosis is personal. A man insignificant in civilian life discovers he has now a mission. An enlargement of his nature has taken place. But it is a civil war, some time of brother firing against brother. The enemy we fire against might be a relative, a school friend, a neighbor and every man has to find his own solution. No one talks about it.

Between the men I feel there has developed a sense of brotherhood. I imagine like the feeling that exists between Alpini troops. That is natural, because it is ex-Alpini who predominate in the First Julia Brigade.

To my eyes every brigade has its stamp. The Julia is unique in many ways: it is the oldest, has the largest number of serious dedicated partisans; it is also the brigade with a partisan with only one leg, a messenger with only one eye and no index to his right hand, and it also has a girl.

Whatever the tone of the brigade, all brigades have this in common: they lack the arrogance of the fascists and the robot discipline of the Nazis.

Last ritual of the day

Max gets ready for bed. He lifts the heavy door off its hinges, lays it down parallel to the fireplace, raises one side with a rock, bundles the English army coat into a pillow shape, lies down and places his Alpino hat over his face.

Thin as a rail, Max is a spindly carcass of brown bones, bony elbows and knees. Now stretched out on the hard surface he won't move until morning. Max is a super messenger. He was never drafted and he has developed his own military strategy. He carries a '91 automatic rifle; he calls 'his trusted one', carries no pistol, only a Balilla hand grenade at his belt. Everyone laughs at the hand grenade. "Imagine trusting your life to a Balilla, man, you're out of your mind."

Max explains to me "For me instead a Balilla is just right, it's what I need. I have to deliver a prisoner in town, on a street corner I find myself face to face with a fascist or a German, a Balilla is just right, easy to extract (with a quick hand movement he extracts it from his belt), easy to throw. It doesn't do anything to him or to me; it confuses him and gives me some time. Right now everyone wants the Italian Mitra, no one wants a rifle or a Sten gun, and for me that's too many shots. I trust my faithful '91.

Every time Max enters town to deliver prisoners to Monsignor, he risks his life. He has had narrow escapes he likes to tell Ailù about. He has a charmed life. Is it providence? Or is it his war strategy?

We are so high up we seem suspended in space and feel light headed. The sky today has lost all color; it's a luminous ostrich shade. In the distance the line of brown peaks and the blunt top of Molinatico are a cutout of heavy cardboard. We can see the roofs of home, the two bell towers, and the river. The red tiles of our roofs are set like gems in the emerald green of the trees. We follow them in our binoculars along the streets, past each house until we recognize the red tiled roof of home.

A little old woman comes to the camp. She is as dark and dry as a smoked anchovy. Dressed in a rusty black cotton dress and apron that reach to her ankles, she wears on her feet a pair of man's shoes without laces, on her head a black cotton kerchief. She stops; curiously she looks around, at the circle of card players, at the men sitting around, at the iron pot simmering on the fire. She takes her time before asking: "Is Commander Gek here?"

Gek gets to his feet slowly, smiling benevolently.

"I am Gek. But Commander I am not. And so, good woman, what can I do for you?"

"Signor Gek, the Englishman, the tall blond man, you know him? But yes, you know him; he is here with you, here in the camp. You see, Signor Gek, the Englishman comes every day to my house to buy eggs, but when it comes to paying…"

"But, my good woman, we can't pay for the eggs Captain John eats. You know that, you understand that yourself, don't you?"
"No, no, imagine, that's not why I have come. You see, the English gentleman pays every time with a thousand liras note, and, signor Commander, I don't have the change for a thousand liras, I will never have the change. But you, you can make the change for a thousand liras, Signor Commander for the English gentleman?"

"That I can do, nonna, that I can do. Gek smiles, places his arm across her shoulders, pushes her toward the path. "Go, nonna, go, I will take care of it." And he sends her off reassured.

Gek knows and all of us listening to him know that Captain John not only loves the old woman's eggs, but her hens as well and pays them an assiduous court. He lures them away from the farm yard with handfuls of corn, and takes them for walks out of sight of the farmhouse. The hens follow him pecking at the corn. At a safe distance the captain falls flat on his stomach, makes enticing sounds in English while the hens peck and cackle, they squawk vexed at the throw of the lasso, and having finished pecking the corn make their way home. Back to the hencoop to make the eggs that the captain goes to buy. All of us listening know this, but Gek has not told the old woman. Perhaps out of consideration for Captain John or to spare the old woman.

The hens are in no danger. Captain John is not an expert with the lasso.

"What do you expect from that poor devil?" Ailù is talking about a student. 'The poor fellow will never be a soldier, what common sense he was born with, he has lost in books. Books befuddled his brain."

Like the country folks Ailù is suspicious of books and people who, as he puts it, use long words and don't speak the dialect. I speak Italian to Ailù but he answers in the local dialect. The rough sounds seem just right for him. Unlike the farmers Ailù is not a pessimist .He is satisfied with his life, he takes the good and the bad and punctuates his days with glorious bouts of drinking. Fate is his friend.

The peasants here live to complain, suspicious of everyone and even more suspicious of a generous gesture. Everything conspires against them, they feel. Nature, the gods of rain and drought, the poppies in the wheat fields If one of them is asked a simple question, he is too smart to give a straight answer.

They watch us with curious, suspicious eyes. They don't like us.

Yet a change has taken place in their life.

It needed the wave of German violence to wake them up. They saw their land devastated, their property ravaged, their clothes strewn with contempt along the hedges and finally realized they too were involved and had to find a solution.

It was a serious step for them. They finally realized the only way out was to join and be part of the Resistance.

For the peasant it was a big jump in civil consciousness, to acknowledge finally the collective experience of the times and forget his own selfish interests.

The ones who have joined are serious soldiers. Fully armed, they have discovered an unexpected courage and a new dignity.

"Let's go, says Ailù, you'll have something to put down on your scrapbook. I promise."

We are going to pick up a fascist sergeant home on leave. Ailù who is well informed on him has discovered that he has brought his Mitra with him.

The mule sets the pace. It will take us over four hours to get there. It's a farm house with a new stable and a well tended vegetable garden.

Hidden at a safe distance, the mule tied to a tree, we sit and wait.

Finally Ailù gets to his feet, and we approach. The woman who comes to the door has a baby in her arms. Another little boy, when he sees us, hides in her skirts but peeks out with one eye. The woman's hair is gathered on her neck in a tight bun, she has a wooden expression but her eyes are very much alive and intelligent.

"He isn't here," she says quickly. Too quickly, she has seen us approach and knows why we have come.

"I know he's here." says Ailù.

"Keep your gun on her, shoot if she moves." he orders me.

He opens a door, takes a look in the room, goes upstairs, comes down, starts opening drawers, cabinets, gather salami, hams, small round cheeses, bottles of wine and piles them all near the entrance door.

"I don't buy it, he's seen us coming, I know he's here." He stares into her eyes. "Tell him ...no, he knows he's seen us...he knows what to expect…tell him to expect me."

The woman doesn't take her eyes from the ugly big gun (from me she has decided she has nothing to fear), she counts on her cunning, she knows that one wrong word, one move from her could set off that wicked gun and she is careful not to provoke him.

Now we follow him upstairs again; he opens the top drawer of a chest, scatters all the contents on the floor, kicks papers, letters in faded ink, photos; he examines some sheets of Treasury stamps, drops them. "Don't take them, please." the woman asks. He goes on kicking everything around his boots. "Tell the bastard..."

He pushes her downstairs, picks up a stool, throws it against a wall, and stops at a loss.

He knows the man is hiding, but what can he do? He starts toward the entrance, past the heap of loot he has piled there and walks out. I follow him.

He is pleased with himself.

"Did you see ..."

We haven't taken the sergeant or the Mitra, or any supplies. He has frightened the wife to frighten the sergeant and let him know he's after him. He laughs to himself.

For him it has been a successful visit.

On the way back the mule stops, points its hooves and sits down. Ignoring Ailù's heavy smacks on her rump, she won't budge. I expect Ailù to get angry and start swearing, but he too sits down.

"You want to take a rest… well, rest a while, you poor beast." He has just sat down when the mule gets to its feet and starts out. Ailù takes the bridle, and pulls her forward.

Lower on the steep hillside the farmer has burnt the grass, the slope is black with burnt stumps and cinders and we have to walk through it. We get to camp in a sorry state, our uniforms black to our knees. No Mitra, no supplies, but Ailù is satisfied.

A day's march across the hills to try a Bren Automatic and make a halt at Porcigatone where shoemakers are busy making boots for us. When we enter the village children run out to see the horses. Dora and Pina seem to enjoy the admiration of the children. They are beautiful horses with long, blond manes and heavy tails, a star on the forehead. They look like twins but are not friends. When the children get close they kick, snort and carry on. We have learned during the march that Dora has to be allowed to precede Pina.

Evening is sad in the hills. In the soft yellow green light it's then that we think of home, of lighted rooms, dinner tables, fresh sheets on the beds. A dog barks, other dogs across every hill answer. It's a melancholy sound. The evacuees from the city seem to feel it too. Without energy they sit on kitchen chairs outside the houses in the hush of evening; they don't consider their stay a vacation, they wait to return home, to the comforts of home. Here they live in makeshift lodgings, crowded in living quarters without conveniences, no running water. The rooms are bare and depressing with smells of apples, grease, and mice.

Seated on a kitchen step a young mother reads aloud to her two sons pressed on either side of her, their hands sunk deep in her lap. It's a love story. A book without illustrations, but the two boys, eyes on the mother's lips, listen enchanted to the gothic tale of love and death.

All around is heard the sound of insects, the croak of frogs, and, loud above them, the cricket. In July the cricket seems to be in love with its song, monotonous, persistent, it's heard from every bush, tree, every hedge. It is a synchronized love song, an insistent thrill beating in the veins of the hills like the sound of the world turning.

On the return march the column moves slowly. Below us fireflies trace their aerial moves above fields and meadows, all at the same height it seems. In the distance is the flowing brown line of the mountain ranges. Someone starts to hum, someone else joins in, and it becomes a chorus, low and slow as a lullaby.

'Stelutis' The Alpini *chorus*

Against the immense reach of the sky, men and horses are silhouetted in the darkening hush of evening. Dragotte gets off the horse, raises his arms, pulls the voices together, directs.

It is a deep stupendous chorus, the chorus of 'Stelutis'. It is a chorus every Alpino loves.

We sang it in June on the death of Sam.

Sam, a dear friend, was a brilliant student of medicine. It was his last request.

"Together, sing Stelutis" for me. One last time together sing "Stelutis".

Sam's Requiem Hour.

Punteria has gone. He has left the First Julia Brigade to join one of the Beretta Brigades. His departure is a loss for the Julia. For me it is a great loss. I will miss him very much. Something romantic, adventurous has gone. He transformed each attack into an adventure. He saw the fascist enemy as a Red Indian, an Indian brave, for Punteria wanted the enemy too to be heroic.

At camp, like a cowboy he would practice for hours with his Mauser: he would draw, aim, and shoot as he had seen cowboys do in western films. That's how he got his name "Punteria" "Aim". For the fascists he felt no particular animosity. After all, he would say, we too have been educated into it, we too have worn a black shirt, marched, shouted 'Duce, Duce'. The only difference is, we came to our senses."

The Militia men we went to disarm had grown up with us; many were school friends. Once they were caught, disarmed, made to tear their black shirts, he was anxious to be rid of them. He made them undress and sent them home in their underwear with a piece of advice. "Go home, idiot, think about it and wake up."

If he knew him to be a convinced, obsessed fascist he would hit him on the forehead with his open palm, shouting repeatedly: '*D-U-C-E D-U-CE*' till the man's head started spinning.

My baptism of fire, the raid at the station had all the romantic elements Punteria wanted: the blonde moon riding high in the sky, the surprise in the timing as the commuter train was waiting to pull out of the station, the forlorn sound of a goods train whistling out of the tunnel. If these elements were missing, Punteria supplied some of his own.

Another raid at a small station was routine, not exciting at all for Punteria, so he added his touch. "You dress up as a girl, he said to me, go and talk to them, get them to talk. For the dress, I know where to get you a dress. Just imagine their faces later when they recognize you among us...."

Punteria, was our musketeer, our Robin Hood, the last romantic.

We go to a farmer's house to listen to Radio London to hear the airlift messages.

London Speaking- Positive or negative, punctual at 20.30, the messages come.

Doors and windows are closed; the sound of the radio lowered; the family and the partisans sit in silence. The kitchen smells the same as all country kitchens: of cheese and apples and the aroma of the mash for the animals simmering on the stove.

I wonder who writes these messages?

Italian or English, surely it must be a poet.

From the River Thames to the River Taro, the foreign voice comes speaking Italian, connecting us to a strange world speaking another language. Parla Londra, London speaking.....

The courier of Lyons.
The gate is open.
Ciao, Mariù.
A peach tree is in bloom.
The road is dusty.
John loves Mary.

Confident, the soft voice crosses water, countries, and armies.

Farewell to the hills.
The girl is very ugly.
It is the end of the world.
The mess kit is full.

The Nazi-fascists too listen to Radio London. They too have a message for us. The message of the fascist vice-Secretary of Genoa Spiotta reads: *All traitors will be shot. Young or old, irrespective of age.*
Kesserling's message to all simply reads: *All traitors will be shot.*

Following the positive message, we go to Prato Piano to light the prescribed fires. The wood stacks are ready, the holes dug. Punctual at 20.30, the plane comes, a red eye in the sky, closer and closer; the motor louder and louder, it leaves, comes back, circles around, again leaves; returns and drops its cargo.

The drop brought 20 kegs of firearms, ammunitions, English army uniforms, cigarettes (Capstan, Players), English chocolate.

The age of miracles is not past.

An invitation to tea

Two sisters, evacuees from air raids, invite us to tea. They don't have to repeat the invitation. Corrado loves cakes; I love English tea and the tea ceremony. Dragotte is indifferent, for him, he says: 'tea smells like hay and tastes the way it smells.'

We arrive punctual to the minute. A very beautiful lady opens the door. A vision, tall, slender, a delicate porcelain face, to our eyes accustomed to the sturdy dimensions of country women, she seems a vision. Enchanted, we stare at her. She is like the fantasy ladies one dreams over in a fashion magazine. The sister too is beautiful, an Egyptian figurine with slanted eyes in a tanned face. But inevitably it is to the older sister's face that our eyes turn. Only Corrado is immune to all this beauty. Corrado is engaged to be married. We feel clumsy in our wool uniforms, guns, our heavy boots placed near the ladies' bare feet wearing sandals. The older sister directs the conversation. She moves like a lady, speaks like a lady, crosses her legs and notices the effect on Dragotte. The younger sister sits silent, perhaps she's bored.

"My husband is very ugly." says the lady.

The unexpected observation hangs suspended in the room. Suddenly, as if the absent husband had appeared, we feel his presence among us in his sea captain uniform.

Later when we take our leave, I have the impression that we take leave of him too standing in spirit behind the delicate shoulders of the lady.

We are invited again.

"Really you must come back, I will make one of my very special cakes." says the lady holding Dragotte's eyes.

"It's a very special cake."

We have to move.

Dragotte has made Captain John head of the Saboteur Group. This is his first assignment: to guard the eighteen prisoners on the march.

We know very little about Captain John. Only that on a mission over the Apennines his plane was shot down and caught fire. He chose to stop with our group after trying other groups. He sleeps with his boots on, his rifle at his side.

Now, a notebook on his knee, he makes his plans. The saboteurs sit around him in respectful silence. Being made head of the saboteurs hasn't changed Captain John at all, he stays what he was, a distant and reserved Englishman with his own English ways. But in the saboteurs the change has been extraordinary. D'Artagnan, Napoli, Jim, proud to have him as 'capo' have taken on a new dignity. Captain John is a model of military stiffness. The kind of chief the saboteurs needed for they are dedicated but restless and troublesome. It's not clear how they understand Captain John for he knows only a few words of Italian. It doesn't seem to be a problem. The saboteurs study his face, grasp what he wants to say and supply him with the words he needs.

Before starting out Captain John orders them to help the sick prisoner up on a mule.

We move to Mariano.

Finally we have an office, two rooms above a kitchen where Ailù does his cooking. The rooms have wooden floors; the outside stairs too are wood. In the first room we have placed a table, two chairs and a typewriter.

I learn to type. With difficulty I make a list of all the prisoners' names.

The prisoners are a sorry sight. One day thinking of improving their appearance, I have an idea. We have three barbers in the camp available and as barbers they are mostly unemployed .

"Why don't we have the barbers shave the prisoners? " I suggest to Dragotte." They will look and feel better shaved and cleaned up."

The barbers protest. The prisoners would not feel better. The beard, the barbers say, is a protection against sunburn. But they consent to shave the prisoners. A terrible idea, never again repeated. Lice, before hidden, now travel freely over their sad bare faces, which even in the heat seem blue with cold.

The sick prisoner is much worse. I am afraid he will die,

"Let's send him down to Monsignor." I suggest to Dragotte.

"What next? Send Max to town and risk his life for a German?"

But later in the afternoon I hear him ask Max. "Max, it's up to you, it's not an order. Do you want to go to town and deliver him to Monsignor?"

"Sure I can."

We stand looking at the poor man stretched out on his side.

"But what about him?" says Max. "Poor devil, he's in bad shape."

But later in the afternoon Max and the prisoner leave on foot. The prisoner has no shoes; his feet are wrapped in rags.

On his return Max presents the food list to Corrado. It reads:

> 1 flask of Red
> Bread
> 2 sausages

Corrado reads it and frowns: "One flask of red is that much wine necessary?"

Max's answer is always the same: "Does a car run without gasoline?"

This insistence of Corrado on Max's drinking, both Max and Ailù find unnecessary and trite. For the men wine is as necessary as food. More, wine is food and lifts the spirit, as Max insists." "A glass of wine to start the day would be just fine."

"Two sausages? Why two?" Corrado asks.

"What else? Do you expect me to sit down and eat with a dying man watching me?"

"So, you buy sausages for a German prisoner?"

"The priest wants to see you." says Max.

"Does he want to give a sermon here?"

"What makes you think he wants to read you a sermon? He's waiting for you at the old woman's house."

"Max, can you think of another reason why a priest wants to speak to me?"

"Go and see what he wants, he's a good fellow."

Before I can change my mind, I take my cap, my gun, cross the other room, and run down the stairs.

The old woman opens the door. He is sitting in the kitchen. He has gray hair, the rough hands of a farmer open on his knees.

He rises, moves a chair forward, moves another chair, he is embarrassed. After placing the rifle behind the door, I sit down.

"The partisans stay away from the church" he says after I am seated. "They never come to hear mass, yet they have the time, they have plenty of time on their hands. In fact, they have too much time." Silence

"This Sunday is our feast day. There will be High Mass, singing, a procession; our Lady will be carried out in procession. But it's a pity, her cloak is worn. A shame really, the cloak is falling to pieces."

Another long pause

"There will be singing, it's true that our singing, well, down in town you are accustomed to hear better, your High Mass is better. All the same it's not so bad; after all it's the same, a song in praise and glory of God and the Virgin, the same song. And the statue of the Virgin is very beautiful."

He sighs, looks at the dust on his shoes, the edge of his black cassock.

"The cloak is green and violet, the nuns embroidered it with gold thread, but now it's falling apart."

He hesitates, lifting his eyes, our eyes meet and he says quickly: "Signorina, forgive me, I thought you might use your influence. If you asked them, they would come to mass and to the procession. Forgive me, if you asked, they might come Sunday…It's true, the mantle is in a very bad state, very bad…."

Now he has finished talking, so I have a suggestion to make. "We have parachute material, some white cotton and some green nylon, a very thin light nylon. Do you think the green nylon could be used? I don't know, I have no idea if it would be suitable. Could it be embroidered for the mantle of the Madonna?"

Now he gets to his feet. "Yes, yes, I have heard it is strong material."

"Beautiful" he adds: "strong material. It would be a solution. Certainly, it would be a solution…"

Now he is all smiles.

Before I leave, we shake hands cordially.

My suggestion to go to mass for the feast of the Madonna is not a success. Dragotte is away, Corrado is away too. Ailù looks at the ladle in his hands; I can see that the very idea of entering a church embarrasses him. Boris and Birichino have kitchen turns, Candidus for once is silent. Max has a hole in the seat of his trousers.

"All right, all right, do as you please but on Sunday I intend to go to church."

Then I remember that Napoli and D'Artagnan are courting girls in the village. Napoli has even gone to town to a hairdresser's for a permanent wave. I go and look for them.

"Come, let's all go, it's a special day, lots of good things to eat." I say, "The girls might invite you to their big dinner."

Ready to leave on Sunday we are seven.

We have washed our faces, washed the mud from our boots, rubbed them with rags. We feel festive. Hair brushed and still damp, we are presentable. We leave in Indian file fully armed.

When we arrive in the church square some young men leaning against a wall stand watching our approach .Mass has already started, but they don't enter the church. In their heavy black suits they too look festive.

It is an odd thing: the peasant working in the fields wearing his fustian clothes the color of the earth looks in tune with his background, dressed in his Sunday best, he becomes gawky, he discovers he has hands and feet and doesn't know where to put them.

The young men don't take their eyes off us as we cross the square and climb the church steps. At the door the saboteurs slip their

Mitras off their shoulders and take off their cap. I take off my cap, but quickly I put it back on my head, and we enter.

Women and girls sitting on the pews turn their heads. The young girls immediately pretend indifference. Unsuccessfully, with the entrance of the saboteurs the atmosphere inside the small church has changed. It's felt like an electric current. They start fussing with their veils, straightening their shoulders They sit up straight. Their rigid backs are a silent message -- a love message.

To dance in the evening they send for Fischietto. The music from his accordion brings good cheer and, I am told, his presence too. And this is a mystery, for Fischietto ignores everyone and everything around him. Fischietto has come to play. Fischietto and his piano accordion are an institution for as soon as he is seated, head lowered, eyes closed, bent over his instrument Fischietto starts to play.

He ignores the glass of wine at his elbow, lost in a trance Fischietto plays. Listening to the sounds his fingers draw from the keys, his right foot beats time to the music.

The air in the room gets thick and heavy, thick with cigarette smoke and odors of heated bodies sweating and swaying to the rhythm.

Without stopping Fischietto plays on.

The dancers go on dancing all night long.

NOTICE
Passengers traveling on the line
Parma-La Spezia are not allowed to get
down at the stop Borgotaro. Any stop
in Borgotaro is forbidden.

"Ailù, do you want to know the story of the gifts I have received?"

"What gifts? Where do you keep these gifts?"

"I said the story of the gifts. By now who knows where the gifts are. Now listen.

The first I received at Tomba. Some of you, my brother Aldo and Punteria and you among them had gone to Varese for a raid.

Punteria brought me a book - *Gone with the Wind,* a big tome of many pages. I thought if I ration my reading, it will last me weeks. I never even opened it .The Easter attack came and the day after Easter the Brigade left Tomba. I had to go with you and the book was left at Tomba. I remember in the attack you caught a spy. He was a fascist informer who traveled around peddling spools of thread and needles from a box around his neck. He had a pair of woman's shoes and someone put the box in my hands. They were ugly yellow, plastic things. I placed the box by the fountain where the village women came to wash their clothes."

"Why didn't you keep them?"

"What for? I had a good pair of skiing boots on my feet. And then, a dead man's shoes…At Linari someone brought me a small bottle of Chanel Number 5. But the stopper was stuck and the bottle couldn't be opened. Well, I thought one day when I get to take a bath, I will break the bottle and perfume myself from head to toe. That too I lost

One thing I still have: a small volume of Salvaneschi. A partisan from another group had taken it from a fascist and before giving it to me, wrote on the fly lead.

"Involuntary gift from a fascist adversary to a partisan…"

I also received a lovely Swiss wrist watch, a Longines, but the clasp didn't work. Remember when we hid in the river in a fog so thick we couldn't see our noses, and the Germans firing all around us, I asked you: "From where are they firing?" and you knew I was scared, and you said: "It's all right, we can't see them but it works both ways, they can't see us either." I lost the Longine then. Probably a German found it. They collected watches, the Germans

Now that I think of it, the only gift that was any good to anyone was yours."

"My gift? I've given you a gift?"

"Don't you remember, not so long ago, a packet of tobacco."

Candidus standing by the fire bursts into one of his rough laughs. "That's rich, that's really good. Let's hear the story of the pouch of tobacco, Ailù."

"What have you got to do with it, you…?" Ailù tries to reach Candidus to kick him, but Candidus takes off quickly around the corner of the hut. Ailù with the ladle in his hand follows him. When he walks back he grumbles in a temper, puts the ladle in the pot, and starts fussing around the fire.

"Well, Ailù?"

"Well what?"

"What was wrong with the tobacco?"

He sits down, opens his ugly switch blade knife.

"We know who gets your ration of cigarettes." He adds: "You have gone around too asking the women for socks for them, and the farmers don't like it. You forget that they are Germans because they are hungry. Me, I couldn't care less. Just remember, they don't forget either."

"Ailù, was it tobacco in the pouch?"

"Tobacco? Yes, it was tobacco." He laughs. "But not for smoking, nothing they could smoke. Not tobacco your friend with the canary yellow face, l'Amico Fritz, could smoke …no way…Moldy, moldy through and through."

A baroque character is Ailù. Who can understand him? Ailù's logic is as complicated as the reasoning of the peasants. How old can Ailù be? It is impossible to imagine him young, or old and decrepit. He seems to have reached the age right for him: the age of a soldier and a serious partisan. He is driven by one consuming passion: an obsession of passionate hate for the fascists. What affront can he have received at the hands of the 'black shirts' to make him so vindictive and cruel?

This is one side of his nature.

But there is another side to him: a gentler side Ailù hides as if ashamed.

Ailù reminds me of some of these old women we meet up here. They stare at us, listen not to what we say it seems but to what we're thinking. They seem to absorb from some primitive depth what we're thinking. Merry old women, dried out and toothless.

They have shed their mask, life is hard, make what you will of it, it's a daily struggle, so, why fuss? They speak the dialect and are not impressed by our book learning or by all our guns. Not even the SS seem to impress them.

Ailù is like them. Perhaps this explains his ascendancy over the other men. The men want his approval, they seek it. His approval means more to them than that of the commanders.

This morning the people looked out of their windows curious to know if the railway bridge was still standing. In their sleep last night they heard the explosions, loud and prolonged as the echoing roar of cannon shots. The bridge still stands. One of the holding piles has given a little. The German patrol is out inspecting. Under the nose of the patrol Jim and D'Artagnan last night climbed one of the stone piles to place the explosive on the track. They returned to camp limping and without boots thrown by the blast when the locomotive passed.

These are busy days for the saboteurs (and for the State Railroad System as well). Between the stations 60-61 the saboteurs have blown up locomotives and over 200 meters of rail track.

One night they encountered Bill's saboteurs at one of the bridges. They complained to Dragotte on their return.

"What the devil are Bill's men doing here, it's not their territory."

"They are lucky…"

"We were about to fire when one of them slipped on his backside and swore in Italian."

"It saved their skins…"

"Your brother Aldo was one of them."

"What does Aldo, an ex- Alpino, know of explosives?"

"More than you do. Captain Bernini came to instruct them, they came with 60 kilos of explosive."

"To show us how to blow up a bridge, us poor fools with a few petards…"

The railway bridge still stands, it has given 50 cm. In a few days the Germans have repaired it and the trains continue to pass.

Sometimes a girl asks to join the partisans. Ailù must have approved of the idea, for one day he brings a girl to the camp. We watch the horse, Pina climbing the opposite slope with Ailù walking beside the horse. We are sitting under the burning sun, Candidus, Birichino, Boris and I, dusty, sweating, untidy, hair matted, boots dusty. We are not a pretty sight, in no way ready, or happy to receive visitors. We follow the horse's progress in an unreal silence up the steep slope. We can see that she is very pretty. She sits gracefully on Pina, her elegant brown leather boots come to her knees.

When Pina comes to a stop she jumps down, light and graceful and smiles all around. Her long hair is loose down her shoulders. She is fresh, radiant, pleased to have arrived. We sit embarrassed, conscious of how we must look to her. As if a dark cloud had passed above us, we communicate our discomfort and she too starts to look uncomfortable.

Later sitting on the wood block she holds a tin plate with a ration of food. She pushes the food round and round, her eyes lowered, but she doesn't taste it.

Before dark we watch her leave, her silk blouse is slightly dusty as well as her leather boots. Sadly we follow Pina's slow progress down the slope, unhappy at having disappointed her. We could understand how different her imagination had pictured our life, how different she found the reality.

For several days Ailù is sulky and doesn't address me a word. When he is able to speak he says: "You weren't very cordial to her I must say." "Ailù, as soon as she saw us, she knew she had made a mistake. Would it have made any difference if I had been friendlier?" "She is one of our couriers. Another girl to keep you company, I thought it would please you."

We go for supplies. We start before daybreak and the mule sets the pace. We travel in silence for Ailù has no small talk and Renzo and I don't feel we can start a conversation. At the first stop we find potatoes and small round goat cheeses. The farm vegetable garden is large and well-tended, flowers and vegetables next to one another: a bed of tiny leafed lettuce next to rows of chamomile flowers and small green onions. Near a fence a row of Easter lilies (intended for the church) and a rose bush of large, heavily scented roses that last one day.

The next farmhouse we come to seems deserted; we see no smoke from the chimney which means the women are out in the fields. Ailù knocks, is about to turn away but the door swings open. We go in.

"Go upstairs; see if anyone is there, I am going to the stables." He says to me. In a corner of the kitchen are a few stone steps leading upstairs, I make a quick tour in the rooms upstairs, am about to start down when I catch sight of a figure under some bedcovers. I approach.

Almost buried in the pillow folds is a face, small, wax-yellow with age. She doesn't answer when I speak to her. Her eyes are open but I move my hand in front of them, they don't blink. She hardly breathes.

All the family is out working in the fields.

"Poor woman, says Renzo at my back, "The women are with the men out in the fields, its harvest time."

Let's go," shouts Ailù from outside.

Renzo and I stand still, our eyes on the poor pitiful face. We hesitate.

Ailù's voice calls again.

So we leave her waiting, as we found her, waiting.

Between Ailù and the mule there is a secret understanding. After we have loaded the supplies, the mule starts out and takes us to a wine shop. By a long trail or a short one, we end up in a wine shop. Sitting sideways at the wine stained table, Ailù relaxes. He has ordered a liter of red wine for Renzo, and one for himself. I don't drink wine. A point against me: "How can one sit in the company of someone who doesn't drink?" he asks me angrily.

His elbow on the table, the glass in his hand, Ailù starts with a monologue. It's a prelude that consists of a long imaginative list of damnations and invectives against his hard life, the idle rich, and the hated black shirts. With the second bottle of wine, Ailù's voice softens. Now it comes from inside, it unwinds softly like the silver thread in a spider's body. Ailù reflects on life.

"Three beautiful things life holds: a good wine,
                                                    a good risotto
                                                    and a woman."

After this come his reflections on the mules.

"To load a mule is an art; there are idiots who never learn it. A matter of weight, angles, bulk and also the respect that one owes this animal that no one appreciates. Now don't misunderstand me, I have nothing against horses. Look at ours. Dora and Pina are fine animals, beautiful and all, but in our hills one doesn't ride horseback, it's the mule that wins on these trails. Look how the mule puts down its hooves, like the goat, it steps, makes sure and then goes forward. Day and night the mule marches with sure feet, and you can be sure. Trust him; the mule is your friend."

After the break at the wine shop we stop for the siesta.

Renzo ties the mule to a tree, stretches out on his side, places his cheek on his hand and closes his eyes. Ailù goes to sit in the shade his back to a tree, his hat pulled forward, his beard resting on his chest, Ailù sleeps -- a deep sleep with heavy breathing.

In the shimmer of afternoon the heat brings out all sorts of odors: the dry brush around the pebbly slope, the odor of the mule, and of our bodies; the lice in our wool under vests are quiet and let us sleep. Our uniforms are the color of the earth. Like chameleons we've taken on the color and odor of the earth. We are part of the slope, the hills, seasoned by winds and rain.

Ailù opens his eyes, with his thumb pushes his hat back, and continues his monologue as if he'd never interrupted it.

"Trust the mule. But a friend, are you sure you can trust a friend? That's something else, I tell you, you sit in company with a friend, buy him a drink and after two glasses he starts to get nasty and quarrels about nothing. The least thing sets him off, he wants to fight. If you can't stay on your feet, do you think he'll help you and take you home? After you've been drinking with him if you are not careful, you'll end up in a gully with a broken neck or drowned in the river. But the mule, ah the mule, now that's a friend for you. You can't keep on your feet? Trust him, let him guide you; put your hand on his back. Clippety, clippety on and on, keep close to him, walk, walk, trust him, close your eyes if you like, and trust him. The mule takes you home safely."

The temperature has fallen suddenly. Without a break summer is over and absent mindedly the first flakes of snow swirl around as if uncertain if to settle. But definitely winter is here, and we are not prepared.

"Last night there was a meeting at HQ." says Dragotte.

We are walking between two hedgerows along a country road; our breath is white in front of us. I have just arrived from Cento Croci where I have gone to change clothes, take a bath and get rid of some unpleasant guests in my wool under vest. I feel fresh and clean, my hair, my boots shine. I am happy, glad to be back. I have run most of the way.

"Mother didn't know if to boil or throw away what I was wearing. She said lice was woven into every stitch of my wool vest…'like soldiers on the march, she said.."

He is not listening. Eyes lowered, he looks where he places his feet.

"Gek was at the meeting too."

"You didn't expect me one day early, did you?"

No comment.

"You haven't even told me you're glad to see me."

"Imagine."

"They have decided you will work in town with Gek. You'll start a newspaper."

"A newspaper? "

Another long silence.

"They haven't said anything that could offend you, I assure you, and everyone thinks you've worked like a man, done what the men do. No one said anything that might offend you, I assure you. Gek was there."

"Good, Gek was there, you said it."

"There's so much paper work now, all these lists, reports they ask and Giorgione never there when he's needed."

He stops abruptly, now his voice changes.

"Bastards," he speaks with his hands now, as when he is upset, as if the exasperated nerves of his hands led his thoughts.

"They are bastards all of them… bastards. The bastards were all agreed…You should have heard them…" he waves his hand, like a man, as good as any man… first the compliments, naturally, to prepare for what was coming…" He stops. "Can you imagine?"

He stops, looks at me: "Say something, don't just stands there like a dummy…Cry, swear, scream, but say something…"

"What do you want me to say? That I feel sick?"

I feel my face turning red. I feel ashamed, hurt, exposed. I want to hide. Run and hide. Like a sudden blow in the solar plexus, all my complacency has been knocked out of me.

All this time…I was never accepted, I was never one of them. I was just a problem, a headache.

Dragotte continues: "The way they talked… as if it had all been planned, discussed, heaven knows for how long. They were all agreed…"

"They were all agreed? Who? You say all, all…who wants me to leave the camp?"

"The Commando. Corrado, Giorgione was there, Libero, Lino, Gek was there…"

"I know, Gek was there." I add: "But why?"

Why do I ask? I know the answer.

At first I had tried to notice if anyone resented my presence. I was uncomfortable, cautious, and uncertain.

"The detachments have complained, Battista, Gomel say they never see me. I don't move from camp because of you, I've been neglecting all the detachments. Some have complained they haven't seen me for weeks..."

I am no longer listening, I only hear the buzzing in my head, feel the heat on my face.

I just want to hide. I think of his last letter, now in my shirt pocket…of some lines….." *I must anticipate my departure, I have to see her, talk to her, touch her…"*

"I must go down to town, I have to see Gek. "I say.
"Right now?"
"I have to talk to him."
"Wait a minute…."

In town Gek, sitting at his desk doesn't seem surprised to see me.

He gets to his feet. I drop my pack on a chair and we stand looking at each other without speaking. Everything has changed, we both realize it. There is nothing much to say. I have become a problem, a situation. For my brother I am now an embarrassment.

"What do you intend to do?" he asks.
"What can I do? Find a place and hide."
"Monsignor had offered to help you. He's been after me, telling me he wanted you out of the camp. He could find you a safe place…I could ask him."
"No, thank you. Now I am on my own, I'll look after myself."

I take my knapsack off the chair, let it drop to the floor and sit down.
"I left my pistol and the binoculars at camp." I say. Gek too sits down.

After a long silence I say: "There are two empty rooms in the house in San Rocco, I could hide out there." It is a house we own and rent out and it is now empty.

I add as an after thought. "Netta would help me. I'm sure if I asked her she'd help me."

"Cross the river to the other side? Now you don't make sense."
"To me right now, it seems a very good idea: to hide a hundred meters from the German HQ. There is a curfew?"
"Of course there's a curfew."
"What about the bread stamps, the food rations?"
"I'll take care of all that. Send Netta for them"

During the night I cross the bridge.
As I expected Netta doesn't ask questions.

With the help of her husband we have opened two communicating rooms in the empty house. The rooms have two exits, one toward the street, and the other into open country. We work silently, ears tuned to the noises outside on the stairs. For the blackout, we have darned with thick white thread and hung up an old blanket over the inside shutters. Netta's husband Ernesto has placed a bunk bed against a wall, brought in a small table and two chairs. The table wobbles; we are trying to steady it, when we hear steps on the stairs.

"It's Ernesto coming home from work."

There is a sense of normality around Netta that is inconceivable these days when nothing is normal. It is inconceivable to see her so unflustered. Food is everyone's principal worry. Black market prices have put most food out of reach of nearly everyone but people with money for it can be bought in the black market. For Netta, even the bread ration allowed is a problem. With a son and a husband, the dark, heavy ration of bread allowed is not sufficient. Netta seldom tastes it. On the partisan question she keeps a reserved, sullen silence, an attitude I like. She has three brothers in the Beretta Brigades but doesn't talk about them.

For Netta I am not a problem, for her I am someone in need of help.

She has offered to go to my house in plain view of the German HQ. to bring me what I need; knowing the house might be under the observation of fascists and Germans.

It is nice to sit in Netta's kitchen, an overheated, crowded room with the comfortable aromas of toasted oats and a pot of vegetables simmering on the stove. The older boy's damp clothes hang to dry on chairs around the stove. He sits quietly at the kitchen table doing his homework.

It's nice to hear Netta's soft voice after the masculine voices around the camp. After such a long time it's nice again to sit down to eat at table, sleep between sheets.

It's another thing in my two rooms: the cold comes to meet me, rises from the tiled floors, and comes from the walls. Partially dressed I curl up into a ball between the covers hoping to fall asleep.

All I ask is not to think. Not to think of Dragotte, not to think about what I can't change. To close my eyes… not to think… past the tumbling images of disappointment, hurt, and hope, wait…to forget and sleep.
At last I must have slept.

Men around a table have decided: a girl at camp is a nuisance, a girl at camp spells trouble…perhaps from the very first attack at Tomba when I have to go with them, and suddenly find that my old school friends ignore me now dressed as I am in an English army uniform,, a rifle over my shoulder…"You carry it, says my brother, we can't leave it to the prisoner, but don't get ideas into your head, it's not loaded."… the long march…on and on… forever, will we ever stop….uphill, through bare fields spotted with snow, down slopes, across meadows… on and on now we can't see where we're going…. in pitch darkness… will we ever stop…at last a group of empty houses, ruins, a stove, we stop, light a fire…field mice scuttling along the walls….patrols in and out…suddenly a downpour….water sizzling on the stove from the hole in the ceiling, coming under the door, along the floor, …near me my brother (now his name is Aldo), moves his Mitra automatic…the same Mitra we stored at home, the first precious automatic gun on the kitchen table…the perforated barrel shiny with oil… Elio, skilled communist revolutionary talking, spreading the word all of us now involved, responsible… girls and boys no exceptions. Gek, by now seduced by the party…for him the party is now everything Elio, turning to me: "What about you, what are you studying…Tolstoi, Tolstoi the poet of the Muick, on fascist text books, propaganda, fascist propaganda…says Elio, we are all equal, girls, boys past the old taboos, involved all… we are all the same, men, women says Elio,… equally responsible,…Gek like an echo 'we are all the same, men, women',…..no, Gek, we are not the same…nothing is changed, the old taboo applies.…… woman's place…. restrictions, penalties, denials…nothing is changed…

What had I expected? Had I expected a knight on a white charger coming to rescue me? How to separate the man from the brigade…..

But I don't want to go. I can't go. I am your voice. Right from the start that was my mission, my privilege: to bear witness; to register precisely, faithfully…to register the common man pushed beyond his limit…., the ordinary man in extraordinary circumstances…heroic in action, unaware of being heroic.

That was my mission: to register this tangled puzzle, this anguished dream, hope, this congestion of sacrifice, egoism, opportunism, treachery that is the Resistance.

I am awakened by a sense of danger or is it a burst of fire? I turn the light on. On the table are my textbooks, my notes, the anesthetic that always worked, all I need.

How have I managed to stay away from books for so long?

I get up, put on my boots, and wrap the blanket around my shoulders. I will prepare an exam, maybe two, even if I cannot take them.

Yet I was happy….the moment of love…we were happy, happy and free the two of us under that wide open sky, free to live our strange existence that was no longer strange, but simple.….. simple like the linear drawings of children…each day, each hour sufficient in itself, with no tomorrow…. always conscious of one another without the need to look, on the long march, waiting at daybreak to start out on a mission…..at night sitting with the others staring into the eye of the fire with the eternal chorus of crickets and frogs around us…happy… happy in a lightness of heart that I felt sure would never end…

"Now I recognize you," says Netta," with your nose in a book. I am going out to buy bread. If you like I can stop by your house for what you need."

"Better not, Netta. It's not safe to go near my house."

"Who's going to pay attention to me?"

"Netta, what was the shooting last night?"

"Who knows, these Germans like to shoot. When I come back with the bread we'll have caffè latte."

She takes a quick look around the room. "You could do with another blanket. That's something you can use."

The strange thing was that I was perfectly aware of being in danger within easy reach of Germans and fascists. I was ready to run. Sitting at table, my ears open to any sound on the stairs, the knock on the door, but I did not care. I knew nothing of what was happening outside. I did not want to know about attacks, raids, reprisals. Netta did not bring them up and I wanted it that way inside my bubble…

Then one day out of the blue, mother appears.

"How did you know where I was?"

"Richetto sent a courier. He wanted me to know where you were."

How many others knew, I wondered, if the Cento Croci Brigade knew?

In town during an alarm the men leave their work and hide. Netta asks me then to go with them.

"Ernesto has a good, safe place; go with them. They are taking hostages, you have to hide, go with Ernesto."

But I knew where Ernesto and the men would be: buried in foxholes or stretched out in their temporary graves and I had no intention of burying myself alive.

During an alarm, when Ernesto is hiding with the other men, Netta lets me sleep with her in their bed. The baby is still nursing. Propped up on my elbow I am lost looking at his flushed rosy face. I watch him nurse. Eyes closed, he sucks softly, content, fragrant smelling his pure baby smell.

During the night I am awakened by a sharp blow on the nose. Netta turns the light on. The baby sleeps, fists above his head.. We both laugh.

"You rascal, you start early, says the proud mother, slapping women around."

She turns the light off and we go back to sleep.

I listen to mother and Netta talking about the latest raid in our house.

Netta tells mother: "This time they have taken the kitchen table and chairs and much of the linen. Some Germans stayed in the house during the raid, they burned the wood stored in the cellar, but the clothes, the linens, pots and pans, that's not the work of the Germans…"

Mother wants to go and see. Netta tries to convince her it is not a wise thing to do.

I hear myself saying: "Are you sure? You really want to go?"

What trick of mind, what devil pushed me?

It was an idiotic decision, made on the spur of the moment and as I made it I knew it was stupid and dangerous. It was not to protect mother. Mother alone was in no danger I felt.

I was desperate to get back home, to get inside those walls, just to walk through them. To feel I still had a home. I had been gone almost a year.

In place of the army pants, I slip on a tartan skirt, pull on long black ribbed wool stockings, a heavy jacket, and we start out.

I take mother's arm, and hold it for the snow plow has left the surface of the road covered with a thin layer of ice.

Summer and winter it seemed to me that our house was always cold; now the rooms are freezing cold. The ceilings and the windows are too high, the rooms too large for the furniture.

We find the front door lock broken. In every room the contents of the drawers are overturned, everything: papers, plates, glasses, linens scattered on the floors. In the kitchen, as Netta had said, the table and chairs are gone.

Mother walks slowly from room to room. Head lowered, without touching anything. I realize what this means to her. All the dear familiar things of her well ordered domestic routine,(she handled every object with such concentrated consideration) now all these objects, her icons, scattered around her feet. She moves around them without touching anything. Slowly I follow her.

I wish we had not come.
"We could have spared ourselves this, there's nothing we can do here." I say
She bends, picks up a photo and stands looking at it: Gek's photo, postcard size.
Suddenly I feel cold shivers down my back.
"Let's go, mamma, let's go."
I take her elbow, pull her toward the door.
"Mamma, let's go."
She stops at the front door. "We can't lock up, the lock is broken."
"Please, please, mamma."

They are waiting at the front gate. They are two.
They wait as we walk up the driveway, wait as I pull open one side of the iron gate. I let mother through, follow and close it behind us.
"Ausweis, bitte".
"Your identity card, mamma."
I take her elbow. The two place themselves on either side of us. Their automatic rifles hang from their shoulders. They motion us toward the German HQ just around the bend in the avenue.

In the Commander's office on the first floor a row of kitchen chairs is lined up against a wall. The two wait for us to sit down. At the door they click their heels, salute and leave.
On the Commander's desk is a photo of a woman with a girl eleven or twelve years old. Like the Colonel the woman is tall, thin, faded. She resembles her husband. The daughter resembles both parents.
I try to remember what is known about the commander. He is an Austrian, they say, they say he is well disposed, they say....The

door opens, the soldier who comes in clicks his heels, answers the colonel's question, salutes, again clicks his heels, closes the door. The door opens and the same ceremony is repeated. Now I understand the question

"Das ist das Fräulein?"

"Ja, Jawohl."

The door opens a third time. I can't be mistaken, I recognize the prisoner. Ailù called him l'Amico Fritz. He stood out among the others because of the yellow jaundiced color of his face.

The door closes. The Colonel asks me: "Fräulein, do you understand German?"

I approach the desk. "A little."

"You were a prisoner in the Military Barracks of Santa Fiora; later in the prison of San Francesco, for how long?" He enunciates each word slowly, clearly. I understand the words, but what do they mean? Immediately I think 'he intends to hand me over to the fascist Militia.'

"I don't remember."

He shuffles the papers on his desk. "You were in Santa Fiora from the 10 of January to the 15 of March. What did they give you to eat?"

"In Santa Fiora what the soldiers ate; in San Francesco, soup and bread at eleven."

"Was it sufficient?"

My mind goes blank. What does it matter?

"What do you give German prisoners?"

"When they were few, what we ourselves ate, later…"

He listens with polite attention, I speak slowly. I have to translate, find the words,

"Why do you keep prisoners if you have no food for them?"
"For the exchange of captured partisans and for civilians taken as hostages."

"And the sick prisoners?"

"Only one sick prisoner. We returned him."

"Fräulein, the prisoner died."

"Oh."

A long silence.

"Hauptman died. Hauptman had no shoes."

He stands considering me, as if talking to himself he says: "Tetanus, Hauptman died of tetanus."

Another silence.

He gets to his feet and shuffles the papers on the desk.

"Your mother can go," he says.

My mother sits composed, her hands on the black bag on her knees, the bag that holds Gek's photo. A hopeless expression on her face, an expression I know only too well. She was always anticipating the worst that can happen in any circumstance.

"Mamma, the Commander says you can go."

She makes a face. "Please, mamma, don't look like that. The Commander says you can go."

"What about you?"

"I'll be all right." I sit down beside her.

"Mamma, go back to Netta, she'll get word to Peppino."

"But what will happen to you?"

"I'll be all right, you'll see."

I take her hands and pull her to her feet. She looks at the chair as if to sit down again. "And you?"

"Don't worry about me."

I hug her. Holding her arm, I walk her to the door.

When mother has left, the Commander gathers up the papers on his desk, goes to the door and leaves.

When the door opens again, it's Fritz who comes in. But not the prisoner I remember under the glare of the sun at Ermeleto, like the other prisoners starved and dusty. Now with a crew cut, trim in the brand new uniform of the Wermacht, the ta-pum on his shoulder. He is again one of them. Uncertainly I get to my feet.

"We will not hurt you, Fräulein." He says, "Natürlich."

We continue to look at each other.

"It was I who recognized you."

I think of Hauptman now dead. Hauptman without shoes walking all the way to town on the rough country road. I think of the meal Max shared with him; the sausage Corrado objected to; I think of all of them starving under the scorching sun. All this the Commander too knows.

Then again Ailù comes to my mind and his constant reminder: *'the only good German is a dead German'*....

But it was not so simple. Arrogant, merciless when they were hunting us…but now seeing them starving under the scorching sun… it was not so simple ….and there was nothing we could do.

The partisans were allowed to take the prisoners' boots for the boots were in better condition than the partisans' boots, but it was understood it was an exchange. For the exchange the partisan left his boots to the prisoner. Fritz too had lost his boots which a guard had taken but had not left his boots in exchange and I had intervened. Days later again Fritz was without boots. Self consciously I wonder if he too is thinking of this as we stand looking at each other.

"I knew we would not hurt you" I see that he holds something in his hand: it's a small comb. He holds it out to me with a smile. It's a gift he wants to give me. I take it. "Danke."

Again he smiles and I think: 'It's the first time I have seen a German smile.'

He still doesn't move, hesitating as if he had something more to say and in silence we just stand facing each other.

At the door he turns: "Der Tabak, Fraülein, nicht gut, nicht gut."

Before closing the door in a loud, cheerful voice he adds: "Niente buono tabacco, niente buono…."

Later the same morning they transfer me into town. The streets are crowded with trucks and SS troops moving out. This must be the tail end of the cleaning up operation. We meet men going up and coming down the stairway of the house where they are taking me, Casa Boveri, called in town The Noble House of Boveri. On the second floor the door of a small sitting room is open. His back to the fire a captain is talking in a sharp angry bark giving orders to two men just leaving.

I am pushed into the room and with me half a dozen Italian civilians. The civilians are lined up against a wall. An interpreter comes in, goes down the line.

He stops before each man and asks in Italian: 'Do you know this woman?'

The men look scared and confused. No one has looked at me. Now each man looks at the wall behind me, at my ears, and shakes his head. One after another, to the interpreter's question they give the same answer. No. No one knows me. The captain laughs, a mocking, sarcastic laugh and waves his hand. The interpreter pushes the men out, closes the door after them.

Now in the room there are three officers and the captain. A round table is laid with a white tablecloth, glasses, silver and two bottles of mineral water. The captain asks me to sit down at table, and they all sit. In front facing me is an officer with a long lean face and black button eyes who keeps staring at me. The others look like all Germans, crew cuts, healthy pink faces, steel eyes.

Mrs. Boveri comes in holding high in her open hand a serving plate full of mashed potatoes. She goes around the table, around the captain's chair and stops at my side.

"Excuse me, signorina, I serve you first. Otherwise, why otherwise there'll be none left for you. You have no idea how much they eat, they never stop eating. They're eating me out of the house."

The captain looks at her, a considering, amused expression on his face.

"She'll be the first one in line tomorrow," he says. His cold eyes meet mine shocked and afraid. He knows I have understood. "We'll shoot the signora first tomorrow morning."

He laughs and the others join in and with their eyes follow Mrs. Boveri as she continues to talk while she walks around the table spooning mashed potatoes on their plates.

In the afternoon I am alone in the sitting room standing before the fireplace when the officer with the pale face and button eyes comes in. He places a spool of thread and a needle on the cleared table and approaches the fire. Turning his back to the fire he opens his belt, a pleased satisfied expression on his face. Looking at me he starts to unbutton his trousers and points to the thread and needle on the table.

Behind him the open fire is burning brightly… it would take a very slight touch from my hand, to land him on the flames…. I go to the table, slowly pick up the thread and needle, thread the needle, slowly make a knot…. without looking at the sneer on his face, I approach, bend down. There are no buttons missing…. There comes a sudden noise, voices, and heavy footsteps outside the door. With an abrupt move the officer turns, with his elbow he hits me in the solar plexus and pushes me away.

The door opens; a soldier comes in and after him, one after another, three Mongols. The captain follows them. The officer before the fire, the needle still in his trousers now buttoned, snaps to attention. The other officer orders the Mongols to salute, clicks his heels and marches out.

The captain faces the Mongols for some time then barks a threat. They stand a closed inscrutable look on their faces. I don't understand the accusation, for it must be an accusation, the words come like whippings. In the silence that follows the three Mongols stand unperturbed, stiff and silent.

"Feldwebel" The captain calls out.

The Feldwebel enters, gives an order and follows the Mongols out. With an angry look the captain mutters something to the other officer and starts pacing back and forth. The officer standing before the fire looks straight in front of him. The sitting room is small and after a few steps the captain turns, and turns again, then stops in front of me. He opens his right hand, spreads out his fingers.

"Fünf," he shouts in my face, "fünf prisoners. We ask five prisoners for your exchange."

The room I find myself in faces the river and the cemetery high on the hillside. A Feldmarshal is my only contact with the outside. He has closed the door but has not locked it. He is a heavy man and moves like a bear. Now and again he gives me a look of disapproval. I represent the "Banditen' that he hates. Near the door I try to listen for sounds outside. There are heavy steps, voices, now and again a sharp order, but of the Boveri family no sign of life.

In the room there is a small bed inside an alcove that faces the window. I sit in the middle of the bed, the silky brown spread pulled up to my chin. I think of Ailù's words 'Don't you forget it; there is only one thing in their heads… to skin you alive…' I believe him: the Feldmarshal sends me a clear message: if it were for him, he'd be happy to do personally. I am hoping that as a German soldier accustomed to obey, he'll stick to his orders. My fear of being turned over to the fascist Militia has died down…. I am thinking of this when the Feldmarshal comes into the room. He makes me understand to come to the window. I get off the bed; approach him in my stocking feet,

"Will your friends come to liberate you?" He smiles ironically.

"Will they come from there?" he points through the glass to the two rows of poplar trees on the avenue that ends in the three gates of the cemetery.

"Yes, I point to the avenue, to the cemetery, to the right, "from there" and then I point to the left, "from there too and…"

With a grunt of anger, he lifts his arm, "Ach du …" he is about to strike me; slowly he lets his arm drop. He gives me a rough shove, pushes me away, and goes out.

I have no watch.

I go back to sit on the bed.

The light outside changes slowly.

A long time after, I take my jacket off. I stretch out between the sheets and fall asleep.

Next morning it is the Feldmarshal who comes to wake me. He shakes me roughly and, without speaking, points to my jacket on the chair, my boots on the floor and makes me understand he wants

me to dress and follow him. Outside it is still dark. The town is asleep. The main street is deserted of civilians. German soldiers walk in the middle of the street in small groups of four or five in the way they have. The Feldmarshal walks before me without turning, stiff as a pole, sure that I will follow.
And in fact I follow.

The supply column starts in front of the hotel: big carts drawn by heavy horses driven by Mongols. Where the snow plow has passed the snow is piled knee-high. Long icicles hang from the roof of the hotel. In the public gardens the pines are bent heavy with snow. The wolf on top of the war monument and the twins under him are hidden under a mantle of snow. The Mongols move around the horses loading supplies on the carts. They stop to stamp their feet, beat their arms against the cold. They look funereal in their heavy helmets of black fur. They must be accustomed to cold and snow. I imagine, coming from a country of everlasting winters, frozen plains and howling wolves.

Mongols and Germans are a strange combination.
    When they see us, two of them come forward, stop before us and without speaking, go behind me, take me by my elbows and lift me off my feet. Without any change of expression, holding me lifted off the ground; they run toward the cart at the head of the column and drop me on the sacks of supplies.
    Legs spread apart the Feldmarshal stands watching.
    The two Mongols take a seat and the column begins to move.

The landscape is dreamlike, the silence a dream of padded sounds, muffled wagon wheels, a cloud of steam round the horses' head. Without beginning or end as far as the eye can reach, it is a desert of blinding white snow.
    (Where can Bill, Aldo and the men of the Garibaldi have found shelter?)
The color green is a memory. A memory our green peaks, our woods; chestnut, beech, locust, birch, all the live protective arms that nature

held out to us and we took for granted. Land and sky meet in an unearthly white stillness. The column moves past clusters of buried farmhouses, buildings, haystacks, stables.

Slow, relentless it moves on its mission of destruction.

Now we have come to territory of the 32.Garibaldi Brigade, or is it territory of the Beretta? But it no longer matters whose territory it is. The snow, the cold are the same everywhere for everyone. The freezing wind that whips the column, the horses, the Mongols and freezes our breath is the same that sweeps the distant peaks of the mountain ranges ahead of us. It's all partisan territory: Pelpi, Penna, Tomarlo, Oroco.

A fury of wind, it swirls around us, penetrates our clothes, freezes our bones.

At the crossroads the column takes to the right, the road to Bedonia. It stops at the first group of houses in the main street. The Mongols get down, stamp their feet, and come to help me down. I stumble and they take my elbows again. With impassive expressions they steady me, and walk me toward a corner house. Still holding my elbows they push me toward a door, open it, push me into a heated room, and leave me.

A German soldier is sitting near the stove before a white enamel basin of water placed on another kitchen chair near his knees peeling potatoes. He lifts his head, gives me a quick look of indifference, lowers his eyes and continues peeling potatoes. Neither does the opening of the door, the coming and going of the Mongols bringing supplies interest him.

I approach the stove to warm my hands. The cook now and again stops, looks at his hands, studies his nails, with one hand smoothes the back of his head

His hair is not a crew cut but neatly styled, an almost white blond, his lowered eyes bulge; he has no eyelashes. He is refined; he lets the peeled potatoes drop into the water with such distaste. He must be a hairdresser in his native Germany, or a barber. A civilian comes in with an armful of wood, puts it behind the stove, with his eyes lowered he walks by me, goes to the door and closes it after him. From a large iron pot on the stove comes an aroma of herbs, perhaps linden flowers? This is an Italian kitchen but it doesn't smell like an Italian kitchen.

The cook-barber continues with his work, peels, cuts, and drops the potatoes in the pot on the stove. He stops in front of the mirror, turns his head, as if I did not exist, looks at his profile with attention.

When I feel comfortably warm, I go to the window and look out.

All I can see is German soldiers and falling snow.

When the food is ready, as from a signal, four soldiers come in. They stamp their feet to shake the snow off their boots, take their helmets off and immediately approach the sink and take a plate. Their faces and necks are red with the cold, to my eyes they seem cut from the same mold: heavy shoulders, fat necks, crew cuts, the typical German cut of the head. Each serves himself from the pot on the stove.

No one has looked at me or turned in my direction. I have become invisible.

They exchange observations in a guttural tone I don't understand, lean their automatic rifles against the chairs, place their helmets on the floor, and start to eat. The cook too serves himself, goes to the table, and starts to eat.

I look at them eat.

My stomach grumbles, it reminds me that I haven't eaten since the midday meal with the officers in the Boveri house the day before.

I was so afraid of them, now in this Italian kitchen with five of them who pretend I am not here, I am not afraid..... I tell myself I am not afraid, I repeat, I am not afraid because I am hungry and I want to eat...... I have noticed that at table there is a place set, and an empty chair and I want to eat...., I know they will not ask me to sit down at table... and I have to decide...

As they have done, I go to the sink and take a plate. Silence at the table. I approach the stove and take some meat and potatoes. I go to the table, move the chair, and excuse myself: "Bitte", and sit down.

In the silence they go on eating.

On the tablecloth there is some sliced dark bread. Kneaded through it are some yellow straw strands (straw in the bread of the Wermacht?) There is a pudding too that looks like a very soft pink custard. After they have eaten the meat each one of them serves himself with his own spoon. I too after the stew, take some pudding. It is very good, very sweet, I would like some more, but I reconsider, better not.

The four men rise to their feet, shoulder their rifles, pick up their helmets and leave.

I go back to stare out of the window. The cook gathers the dishes, gives a passing look at his reflection on the way to the sink.

Suddenly outside there is a burst of fire, the staccato of the ta-pum. The cook lets forks and knives drop in the sink with a loud noise. He turns his head, sees I am watching him and stiffens. Fear knows no nationality. And it comes suddenly, I know, for no reason and at times of no danger. A picture comes into my mind: we are crouched in a ditch; Corrado and Sila have just dropped to safety on the other side. The rest of us crouch in the ditch in a row among a rubble of rusty cans and rubbish, the firing is above our heads....and I wonder, 'are the others as scared as I am?' The firing stops, I slide over the rubble, touch a man, "Let's go." I touch his hand again, his head is tilted at an odd angle and he topples over, and the fear is gone.

In the evening I am alone in the kitchen. I am sitting by the stove, half asleep when a rough hand shakes my shoulder. He is a big man with a fresh healthy complexion and mousy hair. He looks at me with that blank stare they have that doesn't see us.

"Kommen Sie."

I follow him upstairs to a bedroom. It's a room with a double bed and mirrors on every wall. It is icy. The cold seems reflected in all the mirrors. There is a heating stove but it is as cold as the room.

The man makes me understand I can lie down. I take off my boots and jacket. I slip dressed between the sheets. He locks the door and goes to sit in a cane garden chair, places his helmet on the floor and his rifle across his knees.

I am about to fall asleep when I feel him approach the bed and softly lift the covers. He has hardly slipped his boot under the covers that with a jump I am on my feet on the other side.

Furiously he mutters a long list of what must be swear words, I only understand Kält, Kält. Furiously, he goes to the door, unlocks it, bangs it against the wall. Lights go on, doors open. He has awakened the whole house.

Now striking the butt of his rifle against the iron railing he goes down the stairs. Eventually a man and a woman come, carrying wood and kindling and what they need to start a fire. Now he comes in with several blankets in his arms. Roughly he orders me back to bed. He watches the woman working around the stove, when the wood has caught and the fire is well started, he motions her to leave and goes to the door and locks it. Under the covers with half closed lids I watch him get ready. He puts two chairs together, wraps his legs in the blankets and lies down on the chairs, his gun by his elbow.

I wait till I hear him snore.

Sometimes sitting near the stove half asleep, I think I hear gun fire, muffled by the snow, the dull sound of explosions. Perhaps I imagine them. Perhaps I dream them when I sleep.

When the food is ready the four punctually arrive. Always the same four, wrapped in a thickness of cold that they bring into the kitchen. They stamp their feet, go to the sink, serve themselves from the pot, sit down.

They consistently ignore me.

When they are seated, I go to the sink for a plate, serve myself and go and sit at table beside them.

"Bitte."

I excuse myself to men in uniform who ignore my presence. Now that I am no longer afraid of them I look at them differently:

they are just men in uniform; expatriates with another national identification. I listen to their table talk which I don't understand. It sounds emotionless, so unlike the heated, noisy exchange (often quarrelsome) of the Militia in the barracks of Santa Fiora.

Do they ever laugh these men; smile to feel the sun on their face?

They don't pretend, they really are unaware of me.

Suddenly I realize I feel an uncanny, trancelike pleasure in being ignored. I enjoy the luxury of being ignored, but what of our collective experience of the raids of the past months? What of the tortuous irrevocability of the violence day after day?

Can we ever erase from our minds those memories?

These Huns, chosen by God, (Gott mit uns.) with all their steel helmets, guns and most secret plans of war, these Huns with all their clicking of heels and Heil Hitlers will for ever remind us of the terrified faces of mothers, the shot in the head, the roar of cattle in burning stables.

Last night I dreamt I was back in prison, back in Parma in the fascist prison of San Francesco.

We are four in the cell. To stay warm we sit up fully dressed between the covers. Renata's sleep is a soft steady snore. Esther now and again gives a long whistle through closed teeth. But Junior sleeps light; her hand is open on the cover, the thin small hand of a little girl. Here all prostitutes under eighteen are called Junior.

Junior wakes cheerful every morning, ready for the day and all 'things bright and gay,' she reminds me of Colombina from 'Pagliacci.' With a powder puff she covers her face with a thick layer of Coty powder, draws a generous mouth on her lips with a cardinal red lipstick and with this painted face she sets out to visit other cells, like Colombina "full of life and dreams and desires." She seldom washes and under her chin is a shadow of dirt around her neck like a necklace.

When she passes the open door of the next cell, a voice calls after her: "Shameless hussy." Another voice adds: "Aren't you ashamed of yourself, at your age running away with an old man? You were born unfortunate."

Junior smiles and continues on her way. Junior lives for gossip. She finds it in Gemmina's cell: fascinating stories of bordello life. She will come back to share happily with us the gems she has gathered. Accurate, faithful reports …Gemmina said…

"Gemmina said: "for men it isn't beauty that counts, it's something they feel near a woman: a mystery, a promise, and an animal scent. Something men can't resist. Brescia has it. You all know Brescia, she's not beautiful but men find her fascinating. She's mysterious, like a sphinx."

"She a sphinx…bah… more like a witch, a black witch from hell…" says Renata.

"Some women have no mystery about them, like the professor, Gemmina says, the professor, Junior looks over at me with a merry grin, now there's no mystery about the professor, she's like a glass of water, Gemmina said…"

Esther with a look communicates her contempt for all this talk. She despises Junior and all of us. She doesn't speak, she doesn't move from her cot. Esther knits. She doesn't allow anyone to sit on her cot. Renata says she's the only one who has no lice. Esther doesn't wash but looks fresh; her skin is like a peach. She is the daughter of a Mayor and works on her own. She is in and out of San Francesco regularly. She goes on knitting until all the yarn she has is finished, then, like Penelope, she tears it all down, and starts all over.

Between Esther and Renata there is an affinity, an understanding they share. Renata is a trapeze artist in her father's circus. She also performs on a running horse. At times she boasts she beat her mother almost to death, at other times she insists it's not true. She contradicts herself indifferently like someone who doesn't expect and doesn't care if she is believed or not.

She exercises within the limits of the cell taking a flying jump from her cot high in the air to come down with her legs spread wide open on the stone floor. One expects to hear a snap, some bones that crack, but Renata is still supple. She turns summersaults with ease.

She says she has lost weight but she is stocky, compact and muscular as a boxer.

Inside this place everything is gray, gray as the iron studded entrance gates, the stone walls, vaulted ceilings and underground passages. Our faces too have taken on a sick shade of gray, the gray of cobwebs, of the trail snails leave in musty places where no air circulates.
It's the over all color of this dungeon that the Duchess of Parma, Maria Teresa, has built for us.

Before falling asleep I try to remember the color white: white linen sheets drying on a line softly swaying in the sun, our bathroom at home, the white wall tiles, the bathtub smelling of soap. In this place the air we breathe too is stale, used up for there is no circulation. We breathe the same air that other women prisoners have breathed in and out before us for decades.

The men's section is at right angle to the women's section and after many tries, Deo has been able to throw a note wrapped around a stone into the women's section. It's addressed to Giuseppina-Not-Guilty. She brings it to me to read for she can't read. She sees me hesitate and laughs.
"Go on, don't be shy, I know what it says, it's always the same thing, I just like to hear it. Go on, read."
Julia has passed for the last inspection. From the men's section comes the sound of a stick striking the iron bars of the windows. From a nearby cell someone shouts a good-night.
"Thieves and prostitutes have a good night, and golden dreams."

In the dream I am standing with Bargiggia against a wall. Volunnia is there and Mattioli, all political prisoners lined up against a wall covered with green seaweed, sea weed that comes off the walls, out of our fingers, eyes, ears, hides our features, our human shape. Green threads that float light in a green sea and we patiently wait for four Militia men from Santa Fiora who now look into the room in wonder...one looks at his foot, it touches the green stuff, he moves his foot, turns, shakes his arms, legs in the green tendrils that fill the room like water in a well where we float, rise light and happy and take the four with us and now they strike out push against the thick inexorable slime in the inexorable silence that is death and we float light and happy and we know that it is death and we carry them with us, all four of them who continue to struggle...

When I arrived Bargiggia from the next cell brought me a metal spoon. "You won't be able to eat the soup with a wooden spoon." she said.

I wasn't able to eat the soup with the stainless steel spoon either. Not on that day, not on the following days. Now it's too late, the smell makes me sick. At eleven when the lunch cart comes, I don't go out in the corridor but the smell reaches me here mixed with the smell of the latrine. Esther and Renata eat the soup; accept the bowls of soup the others don't eat. The bowls are lined up under their cots and as the food cools a layer of red grease forms on top. Esther fishes through the greasy layer with her spoon and peels the potatoes. Renata eats the potatoes and peelings.

A train load of women has arrived from Bologna where the prisons have been damaged by Allied air raids. Looking at the faces of the newcomers, I thought: my God, what awful faces, and was immediately ashamed. Our faces resemble theirs.

There is not enough room for them in the cells and they will sleep on straw mattresses stretched out along the corridors.

A prisoner stands on our doorway talking to Julia. She tells Julia that in Bologna she was a special prisoner, the recipient of special privileges. Julia listens in her usual inscrutable silence...

"I am not going to sleep on the stone floor," says the woman, I want the cot by the window." She stands looking in, then walks up to my cot and stops. "Move," she says and waits. Renata looks at me, waiting too.

"Come then, and make me move." I say.

In the silence that follows the woman looks at Julia, at Renata and again at me. Julia turns on her heels and leaves. The woman follows her and goes to sleep in the corridor.

"A lady in a fur coat has just come in," says Junior in a conspiratorial whisper. "A very elegant lady. Gemmina said her coat is sable. Her husband too has been arrested and is in the men's section. She is the lady of Castel Guelfo and the owner of the castle."

The lady in the fur coat enters our cell. Still under shock, she sits down on the cot nearest the door which happens to be Esther's. To avoid looking at our faces, she looks down at her brown shoes and ribbed wool stockings. Esther glares at her: she has committed the unforgivable breach of the cell's etiquette. She hasn't asked permission to sit down.

Nine o'clock. Air raid. The siren. The light goes out. We wait.

Again the siren, this time repeated seven times. That means danger. The guards come; push us roughly along the corridors and down stone steps. We hear the rumble of the planes above us. Down more flights, along vaulted underground tunnels, uneven flagstones, we are packed in a corner. When my eyes get used to the dark I recognize Rigolette pressed against me and I feel sick. When the siren sounds again, the women move and I drop in a faint. Julia is called, comes and splashes what tastes like vinegar on my face. Gemmina pushes Julia aside, lifts my head, takes a small bottle from inside her dress and makes me drink. The liquid burns my throat.

They carry me back to my cell. Bargiggia holds my shoulders, Renata my feet; they slip me under the covers.

"Have you eaten?" asks Bargiggia.

"I tried but I can't. Now the smell makes me sick."

"Do you know anyone in Parma?"

"Why do you ask?"

"If you know someone and you have money, you can order food from a restaurant and have it delivered. You can have milk in the morning too."

"I didn't know. Yes, I have a friend I can ask. I can do that"

I have dreamt a field of wild raspberries, a whole field of single plants, and each plant in line holds every small leaf, every fruit on show.

I have fainted again. The doctor has come and given me an injection. He looked in a terrible temper. We heard his angry voice along the hall shouting. Now he shouts at Julia. When he has finished what he has to say, he approaches my cot and listens patiently to me. "No, he says in answer to my questions about the purple and blue stains inside my elbows and under my breast." I don't know what they are. They're not what you're afraid of. It's not a venereal infection."

He lifts my right hand, looks at my fingers. "The sores between your fingers are just plain dirt." He wrote something in a pad.

"Ask permission to take a bath."

Before leaving he turns: "Make a written request or they'll pay no attention."

Rigolette has the same stains. Rigolette is my obsession. Day after day I watch her get thinner and smaller. She wears black satin pajamas that hang in large folds around her legs. She comes from Rome. She says she is a refugee, but the authorities don't know what country she comes from, who she is (she is waiting to be 'transferred') or where to send her... She is accused of having infected a whole barrack of Militia.

Gemmina gave me the grappa to drink. She took the little bottle from between her breasts and revealed to everyone the secret we had puzzled over for so long. We had joked about it when we'd catch her looking inside her blouse. "What do you suppose she hides there, a newborn chick?" She was keeping the grappa for her trial that is coming up, someone finally tells us. A minor, a girl of sixteen was found in her house. She knows she's in big trouble for it is her second conviction."

Renata and Brescia had a fight for no reason at all. Brescia is scared of Renata and careful not to cross her, but for some reason she came into our cell. Renata rushed at her, pushed her against a wall, tore the wig off her head, stamped on it, and threatened to throw it in the latrine. On the spot Julia arrives. She stands quietly on the doorway, holding her small shawl clutched to her shoulders. Silent, motionless, she stands looking in.Brescia defends herself as best as she can, pushing, kicking, but who stands a chance against Renata? Eventually two guards arrive, knock Renata to the floor and take her away (singing lustily) and lock her in the punishment cell.

Back in her cell seated on her cot, Brescia holds a hand mirror before her face. She has a beautiful black eye. She touches it gently with her index, gets out her powder puff and powders her face. Her wig shows the signs of the recent battle. Brescia is a puffy blonde, vain and opinionated. She boasts that she was vaccinated on her leg not her arm. "See? Not like the rest of you, I don't have that horrible mark on my arm."

We are all on Renata's side.

The punishment cell is an underground damp cell, cold and dark and at night rats scurrying around step over you when you sleep. The food is, naturally, bread and water.

In these outbursts, violent and sudden, there is a suffocated anger that we recognize in ourselves, but we lack Renata's courage, a courage which we envy her. Everything about Renata is excessive, her lies, her talk, her exhibitions. In spite of this, we all like her.

Another outburst from Renata. This time it is against a lady visitor. We have learned from Junior that the lady has tremendous authority in the running of the prison, and naturally visits us assiduously. During her preceding visit Renata had talked to her, asked to be allowed to help with the preparation of the soup, offered to help wash the vegetables, peel the potatoes, etc. The lady had listened, shown much kindness and understanding, made many promises.

Now as she sees her, Renata instantly accuses her of having kept none of her promises, of having made her look like a fool, and more…before Julia is aware of her intentions, she takes a flying jump from her cot, grabs the lady's hat, throws it to the stone floor as she has done with Brescia's wig, and stamps on it.

It's a small elegant hat, elegant on the lady's elegant head, with small blue birds fluttering among soft feathers. A hat the lady abandons tempestuously in her hurried departure.

On the floor are left torn wings and scattered feathers we contemplate with pleasure. It is Renata's victory. We applaud long and enthusiastically. But for Renata the victory means five more days in the punishment cell.

The restaurant has delivered my meal: pasta, a small loaf of bread, a bottle of mineral water. I also receive milk in the morning.

February the 21. Session of Examinations at Cà Foscari University. I had prepared three exams.

Last night it snowed and today we are not allowed out in the yard. Julia comes for me for another interrogation at Santa Fiora. "I'll get in your bed and keep your sheets warm."

Renata's usual request "You bring me a cigarette, agreed?" The driver of the car that comes for me offers me a cigarette and she expects me to accept it and bring it to her. I place the cigarette in an opening I have cut in the lining of my coat, out of Julia's probing fingers at my return.

But today Renata has forgotten the cigarette in the general excited confusion and uproar.

All prisoners who have served a third of their sentence will be set free.

The news will affect almost everyone: Renata, Brescia will go out, the country woman who has killed her husband and her daughter who helped her, Giuseppina will stay, and doesn't mind. She is accused of stealing rabbits from a neighbor, but is 'not guilty', she says. "The judge himself said so, 'Prisoner- Not- Guilty." So we call her "Giuseppina-not-guilty." She is Julia's spy and a permanent resident.

Many thieves of Old Parma will be set free, a special group: professional thieves, boisterous, resourceful, they laugh a lot, a fat laugh, broad like their dialect. They are afraid of no one, and ridicule with gusto guards and fascists. Some are religious and every Sunday they go to hear mass from an opening where they can hear mass but not see the ceremony celebrated on another floor. They respect every commandment except one. They are closely knit families. The brothers, fathers, husbands too are mostly professional thieves. For them San Francesco is an inevitable but temporary stay. From home they receive packages, food, cakes, wine everything to make their stay less painful. Many of these will also be set free. The 'politicals' (socialists) of Old Parma' will stay. Now in the cells there are more 'political' prisoners than prostitutes and thieves.

Bargiggia, Volumnia, la Granello, la Mattioli, and another two newly arrived, mother and daughter, accused of giving food to an English prisoner are all 'political'.

Mattioli is terrified of the interrogations at Santa Fiora. She is beaten and made to undress. She comes from the interrogation in a daze. At times she lets herself down on the cold stone floor and keeps saying over and over: 'no, boys, no, I am an old woman.'

When I was arrested I had protested with the captain: "But I teach, they expect me in class tomorrow morning."

As if I had not spoken, the captain goes on with his questions: "Where are your brothers? …..and my answer: "I don't know."

"Why all these addresses in England?"

"I have a sister in Scotland."

"Simpson, is that her name?"

"That is her married name. Mrs. Simpson."

"What kind of an Italian are you….you do feel a hero?'

Day after day, its the same.

When I arrived at San Francesco Bargiggia had warned me: "In case you ever consider telling them where your brothers are, remember you are safe, the men are not."

"How can I tell them where they are? I don't know where my brothers are."

Angrily she answered;"I don't want to know, I'm just warning you."

I tried to explain:"Look, students who run off to the hills don't know most of the time where they are going. Anyway they don't stop long anywhere, there are too many informers every where. The Captain knows I don't know where they are."

Day after day the questioning goes on. Seated behind his desk,(he is a small man) the captain knows he looks very important in his shiny black boots and black shirt. Perhaps he is the one who asks the old woman to undress.

Only the Major doesn't seem to enjoy himself, he doesn't ask me where my brothers are. He is stiff, reserved, asks me to sit down, and offers me a cigarette.

"Signorina, we know that your brothers are with an outlaw by the name of Fermo. You think you're helping your brothers, I know. After the snow melts we will go, hunt them down and shoot them on sight. Think about it, you will be responsible for their death. I speak to you as a father. Think about it."

In the fascist HQ of Santa Fiora, I sleep on an army cot under military blankets. Outside in the hall I hear the click of heels, doors opening and closing, I look down into the courtyard, try to sleep. The guard outside goes back and forth, stops at the door, looks through the spy hole. Guard duty is a long stretch, and these proletarians of the new Italian Social Republic get bored and want to talk. They talk through the door, they talk when they bring me my food twice a day, they talk when they take me to the latrine.

I have lost count of the days.

"What were you doing in England?"
"Scotland, not England."
"England, Scotland, what were you doing there?"
"I went to school."

"Why? Where? What is the name of your school?"

"Montrose Academy."

"A military school?"

"A school for girls."

"What are these lists of English names….Simpson…these addresses…"

It was always the same. Day after day.

You feel a hero, don't you?"

He smiles and says: "And if we shot you in your brothers' place?"

Day after day.

Then suddenly everything changes, events precipitate.

During the night I am wakened by a loud explosion and bursts of fire. Lights go on, hurrying of footsteps, shouted orders with opening and closing of doors. There is a sinister sound of guns and heavy marching. At four o'clock two guards come in, approach the window, look out.

"Don't go near the window." Before closing the door one says "This is the work of your friends. He was only seventeen, but we will revenge him, our companion."

During the night a hand grenade exploded and killed a guard in Garibaldi Square. The streets are blocked. In the net an English officer with an Italian identity card is arrested and with him an officer of the Militia. The English officer, G. Beazely is in German hands in the Citadel. His diary is being translated.

And the arrests begin.

The Militia man, Ravazzoni, has killed himself. All this news comes to me with my food. It becomes more threatening, political prisoners from San Francesco are brought to the public square, and shot as reprisals.

Kesserling's message is broadcast: Death to all traitors.

They transfer me to the prison of San Francesco.

Here I see new political prisoners come in every day. Volumnia, Beazely's nurse, comes in, accused of helping the enemy; German officers and an Italian judge have questioned her. She keeps a photo of Beazely and talks about him as a son.

A student just out of the hospital is brought in with her mother: the charge is the same: helping the enemy. When the student sees us, not to look at our faces, she closes her eyes, hides her face on her mother's shoulder.

I too could not look at the prisoners. When I came in I fastened my eyes on Julia the guard's face. Her inscrutable face and receding chin were preferable to the sight of the prisoners sitting on their cots.

A communist comes in, a young woman with a thin face, dark penetrating eyes that look around her with the utmost contempt. She approaches me: "I am here in your cell by special dispensation, she says, I know your story."

Page by page the English officer's diary is translated and the arrests continue.

They call her the Red one, *La Rossa*. She stands out among all the other residents of Old Parma. A socialist, she sells vegetables, going around pushing her cart in the streets. Tall with large shoulders, a small head she carries proudly high, at Mussolini's fall she dyed a dress and shawl a bright red and started out on her route. She was stopped by two fascist guards, who protested about her clothes and tried to overturn her cart. But the two did not know with whom they were dealing. She falls furiously on them, beats the two of them senseless, leaves them stretched out on the pavement and continues on her way.

She is stopped in Piazza Garibaldi, arrested and taken to San Francesco. Three months later they let her go.

Now free, at a railway crossing she stops a train carrying new recruits, jumping into the first compartment she orders all the recruits to get out and run.

Once more she is arrested and returned to San Francesco. This time she knows she will not leave in three months.

Forgotten but not discouraged or subdued, La Rossa waits.

To my written request for a bath, I receive no answer.

Then several weeks later, Julia comes to our cell, stops and shouts from the doorway: "Solari, collect your stuff, you are going out."

Her words don't sink in.

"Solari, do you hear me? Get up, you are going home."

Here I am a prisoner again. But this time it is in the comfort of a warm kitchen.

From outside comes the sound of distant explosions muffled by the snow. When the food is ready the four come in, always the same four. Wrapped in the cold they bring into the kitchen they stamp their feet, go to the sink, serve themselves and sit down, consistently ignoring me. Silent, relentless the snow keeps falling. I watch it slanting down the window panes, will it ever stop?

(Where can Aldo, Bill and their men find shelter in this desert of snow?)

When the four are seated, I go for a plate, serve myself, pull out the chair and sit down.

"Bitte." I excuse myself.

Exchange Solari *Postponed because of the partisan raid* *Exchange 27.1 .06.00 am.* *Please deliver Solari here.* *In the case the exchange is not possible* *At 06.00 the Commander of the place* *Here will take charge.* *Rob R*	*Austausch, betr.Solari* *Wegen Zerspreng der Bandengruppe* *verzögert.* *Austausch 27.1.06-Uhr* *Bitte Solari nach here in Marsch to setzen.* *Falls Austausch 06-00 Uhr noch nicht* *möglich, kannes* *Ortkommandant hier übernehmen.* *Rob R*

The prisoners exchange takes place on the bridge between Borgotaro and the German HQ on the other side of the river. I had expected to see the three German prisoners that the 32.Garibaldi Brigade had delivered for the exchange, but when I walk alone from the German HQ, I see only two black skirted figures waiting on the bridge: Monsignor Boiardi and standing beside him my mother, her black dress and Monsignor's black cassock sharp against the snow. Hand extended, Monsignor walks forward to meet me.

"Is everything all right, signorina?"

"Everything is all right."

Smiling he turns to mother, takes her hand and places it on mine.

"Here, signora, here you see manifest God's mercy" he says to her, beaming as if he were handing her a personal gift.

"The good Lord has brought your daughter back, back to you safe and unharmed."

After the prisoners exchange I have brought mother to Cento Croci, delivered her in my sister's hands. Here she will be as safe as its possible anywhere now.

For me all I ask is to sleep, sleep and forget the past few months. As if coming out of hibernation, a long convalescence, the padded white silence everywhere feels unconsciously consoling.

A few days before our arrival there had been a heavy snow blizzard. The wind had swept the snow in powdery swirls and waves over the rolling slopes to the Pass now blocked. As we drew up in the car more snow was falling and where the snow plow had passed it had left icy patches hazardous to passengers and motors.

Cento Croci is territory of the Cento Croci Brigade, both sides of the Pass under the command of Richetto, a military trained man. Cento Croci is a reminder of a time when every new brigade still had to prove itself, to form its personality. For me it was a more relaxed time, an exciting time when I felt I belonged. Then I was sure I was one of them and would stay to the end. With Richetto I had gone to an attack to a Militia HQ in Varese Ligure. An important occasion and I felt flattered that he had asked me.

On the eve of the attack, I remember the men had stopped at the Pass of Cento Croci, I remember watching them sitting on the floor making hand grenades, watching them tear black cotton into strips, wrapping the strips around the sticks of explosive. I remember the partisan sitting next to me saying with a smile: "That's why we call them Ballerinas, they wear a black skirt."

It was summer then. It was a lifetime ago.

* * *

We were still sitting at table after a meal in the kitchen. Around us the smell of coffee (that bad tasting espresso made of toasted oats we drank during the war) apple peels on the plates on the un-cleared table cloth when we received a visit. Dragotte arrived, on horseback on Dora.

For mother Dragotte was just the name of another partisan. She looked over at me and I could read what she was thinking: 'the man must be mad …on horseback on those icy roads. But for me seeing was a shock, still unresolved the questions.

Too much had happened in too short a time, Now the sight the Alpino hat and officer uniform, the Mitra, the binocular hanging from his neck, …in a flash it brought it all back… Linari, Ermeleto, Malarino…a jungle density of memories….the moment of happiness, the luminous awakenings…… I expected to find it all stored neatly like images in a scrapbook… disappointment, betrayal, regret…. To separate the man and the commander…..the shared commitment, the loyalty of the men…

"For me it was a revelation." Dragotte says.
"What do you mean a revelation?"
"Seeing you in the frame of your family?"
"Were we rude?"
"Rude? You can't be rude to someone who isn't there. You wiped me out."

Did I have an answer? Separate the man from the Commander.

Dragotte continues: "Later I was saddling Dora in the stable and you came to say goodbye. I could see you through the crack in the door. Your little nephew was with you, a serious little tyke your nephew. You all spoke to him as to a grownup. He stopped and asked you a question. "Zia, he said, why doesn't Dragotte have a beard like every partisan?"

You burst out laughing, that fat laugh one doesn't expect from you.

"He is too lazy," you said, the beard is a nuisance. It was too much trouble. Now with this cold the beard freezes and before going to sleep you always have to decide. Shall I sleep with my beard on the covers or under the covers?"

When he leaves I stand watching Dora's hooves sink in the loose snow at the side of the road. Watching him leave, like seeing someone who mattered so much leave and know that we will not meet again, our roads will not cross again.

* * *

Almost a year has passed.

It was a year of relentless metamorphoses of men and events. Brigades have broken up, demoted commanders, elected new ones. Now partisans call themselves socialists, communists, demo-Christians; they join the brigade they find politically or personally congenial.

The bright dream no longer shines so bright.

We know how things will turn out, we wait. It is a time of compromise, intrigue, opportunism. Inevitably even the face of the enemy has changed: a division of Monte Rosa Alpini and one of Bersaglieri has been added to the German Division Göring.

Now in the hills there is room for everyone, stranded prisoners of war, English, Australian, Russian, army deserters; evacuees from air raids in the cities, Fascist informers and spies.

It took the Resistance to bring us back to the hills, for many of us it is a return to our roots.

Huomini vigorosissimi et gagliardi 'the historian calls them, vigorous and bold men. But no one among us wants to be reminded of these rough ancestors that could neither read nor write.

"And at the meeting of the Council the clan of Costerbosa killed five of the Platoni" Years of bitter feuding for the dominion of Borgotaro.

This land was legend at the time of our fathers but before the resistance these feuds between rich lords greedy of power and poor sharecroppers greedy of land were stories far removed in time and awakened no interest in us.

The present repeats the past; there are the oppressed and the oppressors. The brutal waves of SS raids have left their strata on our hillsides and we are like future fossils, we will be buried to be later exposed by future generations. Geological and biological strata with all our supplies of bombs arms ammunitions and our victims: partisan, fascist, German.

With the imminence of the Allied Offensive, all partisan commanders will meet with Allied Officers at Gravago on the 3rd of April to establish a general plan of action for all Brigades. To the First Julia Brigade is assigned ....the elimination of the German HQ and the occupation of the town of Borgotaro. To the Gruppo Val Taro the elimination of the German HQ of Valmozzola

On the eve of the final attack, I turn up at the camp. What made me decide to come back?

Self indulgence? To placate old ghosts? Or to ask forgiveness for my many sins of omission?

Or was it simply to write 'FINIS to my notes'?

I find Libero, Corrado, Lino, around the fire. Boris too is there, and as I had expected, Ailù..

"Look who's here." Corrado says. He grins broadly: "And how are things with you?"

"Ciao, Corrado."

Ailù raises the ladle out of the pot and waves it at me. "You certainly took your time to get here."

Then he adds: "So you've come for tomorrow's celebration?"

"Will it be a celebration?"

"You can bet on it."

With that thick beard covering his face, it's difficult to know if Ailù is smiling, but I feel he is glad to see me and immediately I feel glad I have come. Libero is amused and that pleases me too. It is as if I had returned after a short leave. No one seems surprised to see me. I have no pistol, rifle or binoculars but I am wearing the dusty English army uniform, and wool cap. I go to sit near Libero who goes on with what he was saying when I interrupted with my arrival.

I knew very little of the plans for the following day.

Of the crisis in the Julia Brigade I knew that Dragotte had been deposed. Libero was now the new commander of the First Julia. Dragotte, Gek, and other old faithful had formed a new group: The Val Taro Group.

"Segretissimo."

That's what is written on the plans sent to every group commander. But, as it happens in all things human, the plans are no longer secret thanks to a talkative partisan and his girl friend friendly to the Germans. The Germans are informed. The attack will not be a surprise. The troops scattered in the various houses around the German HQ have been ordered to HQ, the ones stationed along the railroad tracks are gathered at the railway station and inside the railway tunnel.

The weather too seems to conspire against us. Visibility is poor due to a thin, insistent drizzle and a sharp cold wind. Both contribute to a slow start.

Planned for 4 a.m. the first mortar shot is heard at 5.30 a.m.

A good shot close to the target. It will remain the best shot of the day.

The ground has become a mud trap and the mortars sink more and more making it difficult to control the direction. Two assault teams start out from San Rocco, and two Bazookas. Over 13 shots are fired in less than an hour.

Now the firing is from every direction, the church of San Rocco, the Castle, and the old mill and, loudest of all, the ear splitting sound of the Bazooka above the Electricity Supply Station. Before dawn the saboteurs had crawled to the walls of the building to place their charges. The charges don't explode.

Baffo with the heavy machine gun is stationed close to the cemetery gates. The two of us are sitting near him and Ailù is getting more and more impatient. We can see nothing of the action lower down the hill. We are blocked.

"Not much to cheer about if we stay here" Says Ailù.

After a while he adds: 'Listen to me carefully- we have to get down to the Electric Plant Station, through those iron gates to the garden walls that run at the back of the houses. It's all exposed territory and Baffo will cover us.....right Baffo? Are you listening, Baffo? We count on you. You'll cover us."

With Baffo's assurance we head for the avenue, bending low we reach the iron gates, rush through them to the low stone wall of the first house. Still crouched we look around and realize that we are blocked again. Across the balconies of the second floor of the HQ building stretch heavy barricades of wood planks from which the firing comes. Baffo's fire is no cover for us. Again we are blocked. Again Ailù mutters angrily to himself..

The rain has stopped. The sky is covered with dark clouds. Beside the low wall we wait.

Only much later when it is dark, under cover of the Breda can we finally move and get to Casa Grossi. Here we find Libero, Corrado and the saboteurs.

Night comes. Red, green light signals come from the railway station answered by the signals from the German HQ. Vampa has attacked the station, some Germans have rushed out taking cover in the railway tunnel and are scattered in some stacks of wood from where both Vampa and Gomel are firing to flush them out.

The German HQ is strategically placed.

It is a massive apartment stone building with two rows of heavy balconies on the front and looks like a bunker. Located midway between the two bridges where the highway makes a curve it offers a view of both sides of the avenue; on the roof a powerful binocular on a stand must have offered the Germans an uninterrupted view of all the rolling hills and roads where partisans moved.

This morning the HQ is silent. Before dawn Libero sets out to explore. He crawls along the low ditch by the house moving slowly.

He finds someone following close in his heels and recognizes Bomba. They come to a high barbed wire fence.

'Give me a hand, Bomba, let's tear it down." They pull, push and finally feel it give way. They feel they have done something.

Back at HQ, they find everyone eager to move. Napoli and Jim have a new load of explosive.

"It's twice the other loads, it will set those off too." says Napoli.

They start out and are just back that the explosion comes; a loud roll of thunder, a long rumble, sounding louder and louder. Surely the entire building must be uprooted. Smoke and dust rise in heavy clouds and when it clears we see an arm from a first floor open window waving a white cloth.

"Good, they give up."

"Yes, they give up but what are they waiting for to come out?" asks Libero.

Now we see that the heavy entrance double doors have been blown by the explosion straight across the avenue. White cloths are waved from other windows. But no one comes out.

But, in the end we are the ones who come out into the open. Libero is the first with the loud speaker in his hand.

He hands it to me: "Rosetta, tell them in German to come out and surrender."

Now other partisans have joined us and we are advancing in a fan shape on the avenue when Libero lifting his eyes sees a hand come out of a window with a bunch of stick grenades tied together ready to throw.

"Down, down," he shouts and rolls over to the side of the road. The rest of us, close to the balconies, throw ourselves down. I put my hands over my ears and open my mouth. The roar of the explosion is shattering. Now as if on signal partisans appear from everywhere. A chasm has opened and in the smoke and dust finally (hands above their heads) some Germans appear. Others surprised by the explosions stir among the smoke in the lower level. Part of the stairs has fallen, the handrail is hanging against the wall and the

Commander is coming down the stairs slowly unfastening his gun belt.

Libero meets him on the stairs, holds out his hand and takes the pistol belt. Speaking slowly and clearly he wants to say something about the attack. I think it is praise. He recognizes me and asks me to translate. I have a feeling he is glad it's over. He seems curious about the faces of the men around him, looks at one face after another, and then he catches sight of Ailù.

"It is him, Fraulein, the one I saw, the one with the beard." He unfastens the watch on his wrist. "I know this will be taken from me, I wish to give it to him." Ailù's eyes are fastened on the Commander's face, but his expression doesn't change. For a moment I almost think he's going to refuse the watch.

"Ailù, he wants you to have it, take it."

We now realize that the Commander is no longer the center of attention.

The crowd of partisans has formed a circle around a Feldwebel who stands apart. His fellow prisoners too have moved away from him and we guess that he is the one who, after the surrender, threw the bunch of stick grenades from the window. After taking the Commander's watch, as if drawn by a magnet Ailù walks over. The circle of partisans makes way for him.

Ailù and the arrogant Feldwebel, it's a moment of recognition. The German's China blue eyes, a doll's eyes, stare into Ailù's brown ones dark with all his passionate hate. The Feldwebel covered with dust, head to toe; Ailù bundled untidily in his rusty uniform like a chestnut nestled in his burr. The Feldwebel feels, knows that his fate is in Ailùs' hands, feels that no laws of war apply. The circle of partisans around them knows it too.

"Get in line."
Corrado's sharp order breaks the spell.

"All in line … Tigre, Bomba, count the prisoners…in line by two. Move, move…garibaldi, start the column…"

Is it really over?

Across the bridge at the railway station Gomel and Vampa and the saboteurs are finishing up. Along the avenue groups are searching the houses that they know Germans have occupied. In the Commander's office another group is gathering papers and documents.

Is it really over?

Is it Kaput this bunker, this obsessive presence that like concentric circles had swept over the town, the hillsides, and the people, touched everyone?

The sun is still a shy trace in the sky, this early morning the 9 of April 1945.

Singing, the column moves across the bridge and enters Borgotaro.

Printed in the United States
123063LV00004B/433-504/P